How to Mediate Like a Pro

How to Mediate Like a Pro

✦

42 Rules for Mediating Disputes

Mary Greenwood, J.D., LL.M

Author of
Award-winning How to Negotiate Like a Pro

iUniverse, Inc.
New York Lincoln Shanghai

How to Mediate Like a Pro
42 Rules for Mediating Disputes

iUniverse books may be ordered through booksellers or by contacting:

iUniverse
2021 Pine Lake Road, Suite 100
Lincoln, NE 68512
www.iuniverse.com
1-800-Authors (1-800-288-4677)

Because of the dynamic nature of the Internet, any Web addresses or links contained in this book may have changed since publication and may no longer be valid.

The information, ideas, and suggestions in this book are not intended to render legal advice. Before following any suggestions contained in this book, you should consult your personal attorney. Neither the author nor the publisher shall be liable or responsible for any loss or damage allegedly arising as a consequence of your use or application of any information or suggestions in this book.

ISBN: 978-0-595-46962-8 (pbk)
ISBN: 978-0-595-91247-6 (ebk)

Printed in the United States of America

347.09
Gr

Contents

ACKNOWLEDGEMENT ix

INTRODUCTION xi

CHAPTER 1   WHAT IS MEDIATION? 1

CHAPTER 2   THE ROLES OF THE MEDIATOR 3

• *Rule 1. The Mediator Sets the Tone* 3

• *Rule 2. Let The Parties Tell Their Story* 4

• *Rule 3. The Mediator Sets Groundrules* 4

• *Rule 4. The Mediator Does Not Show Frustration or Emotion* 5

• *Rule 5. Mediation is Not Therapy; Mediation is Not Legal advice* 5

CHAPTER 3   NEUTRALITY, BIAS, AND ETHICS 7

• *Rule 6. The Mediator Must Be Neutral* 7

• *Rule 7. The Mediator Must Not Have Any Bias* 8

• *Rule 8. The Mediator Must Keep His Personal Opinions out of the Mediation* 8

• *Rule 9. The Mediator Must Be Ethical* 9

CHAPTER 4   OPENING STATEMENT 10

• *Rule 10. Give a Good Opening Statement* 10

CHAPTER 5   HOW TO GET STARTED 16

• *Rule 11. Get the Parties To Say What They Want* 16

• *Rule 12. Find Out If The Parties Want Something Other Than Money* 16

• *Rule 13. Get The Parties To Agree On The Issues And Prioritize Them* 17

• *Rule 14. Get the Parties To Do Their Research* 18

• *Rule 15. Don't Let The Parties Get Bogged Down With Principles* 18

• *Rule 16. Don't Let The Parties Get Bogged Down With the Facts* 19

• *Rule 17. Keep The Momentum and Tempo Going* 19

CHAPTER 6   ROLE OF THE CAUCUS 21

- *Rule 18. What If?* *21*
- *Rule 19. Give a Reality Check.* *21*
- *Rule 20. Apologize If Necessary* *22*
- *Rule 21. Everyone Makes Mistakes* *23*
- *Rule 22. Be A Devil's Advocate* *24*
- *Rule 23. Watch Body Language* *24*

CHAPTER 7   HOW TO DEAL WITH DIFFICULT PARTIES . . 25

- *Rule 24. Don't Allow Temper Tantrums* *26*
- *Rule 25. Explain the Repercussions of Walking Away* *27*
- *Rule 26. Don't Allow Parties to Overreach* *27*
- *Rule 27. Don't Allow Parties to Create Diversions* *28*
- *Rule 28. Explain the Repercussions of the Take It Or Leave it Approach* *28*
- *Rule 29. You Can Mediate With a Lunatic* *29*
- *Rule 30. A Mediator Does Not Make Decisions* *30*

CHAPTER 8   HOW TO CLOSE THE DEAL 31

- *Rule 31. Tell the Parties What Will Happen if No Agreement.* *31*
- *Rule 32. Take a Break* *31*
- *Rule 33. Agree in Principle and Work Out the Details Later.* *32*
- *Rule 34. Try a Trade-Off or Package Deal* *32*
- *Rule 35. Split The Difference.* *33*
- *Rule 36. The Devil Is In The Details.* *33*
- *Rule 37. Get The Parties To Give One More Thing.* *34*
- *Rule 38. Show Parties the Big Picture* *34*
- *Rule 39. Know When To Hold and When To Fold* *35*
- *Rule 40. Mediation Follow-up* *35*
- *Rule 41. The Mediator Should Not Expect Thanks or Gratitude.* *36*
- *Rule 42. Give Yourself a Debriefing* *36*

CHAPTER 9   HOW TO TALK LIKE A MEDIATOR 37

CHAPTER 10   HOW TO MEDIATE ONLINE 42

CHAPTER 11   HOW TO MEDIATE IN THE WORKPLACE . . . 47

CHAPTER 12   IF MEDIATION FAILS, SHOULD YOU GO TO
ARBITRATION? 51

APPENDIX A   MEDIATOR'S OPENING STATEMENT 57

APPENDIX B   GLOSSARY TERMS 63

APPENDIX C   WHAT MAKES A GOOD MEDIATOR? 71

APPENDIX D   DO'S AND DON'TS OF MEDIATORS. 73

APPENDIX E   INTERNATIONAL, NATIONAL, AND STATE
MEDIATION RESOURCES 75

ACKNOWLEDGEMENT

I would like to acknowledge my Mom and Dad, Peggy and Jack, who at 91 and 92 are still mediating disputes between me and my sisters. I want to thank my son John, a lawyer and certified mediator, who has helped me with my manuscript. My daughter-in-law Astrid and John make a great tag team especially when helping me buy a new car. They will soon be mediating with my grandson, Jack. I also want to thank Joseph, who lets me know when I violate my own rules at home.

I would like to thank those who supported me on my first book: *How to Negotiate Like A Pro: 41 Rules For Revising Disputes* and encouraged me to write a second book: Florence Cohan Austin, Vic Austin, Sue Barnes, Astrid Breakfield, John Breakfield, Jack Breakfield, Flo Cancilla, Patricia Day, Kathy Doran, Barry Dubner, Bonnie Dubner, Betty Greenwood, John Greenwood, Marnie Greenwood, Peggy Greenwood, Sara Greenwood, Eleanor Hoh, Marzi Kaplan, Joseph Kehm, David Levin, Vashanna McIntire-Moorer, Janet Palacino, Richard Peterson, Susan Pinder, Lessie Reynolds, Nadine Salazar, Leslie Stein, and Kevin Toner.

INTRODUCTION

have been resolving disputes most of my professional career as an attorney, media-
or, human resources director, union negotiator, labor arbitrator, and grievance hear-
ng officer. *How To Negotiate Like A Pro,* is based on my experience as a union
egotiator and *How To Mediate Like A Pro* is based on my experience as a mediator
 over 7000 cases.

While negotiating union contracts, I noticed certain characteristics or rules in the
isputes that were settled that were not present in the disputes that were not settled. I
arted jotting down a list of these rules to assist me in negotiating future union
greements. As I reviewed these rules, I realized that not only did they apply to pro-
ssional union negotiations but to everyday disputes with bosses, spouses, credit card
mpanies, hotels, banks, car dealers, realtors, and eBay buyers and sellers. That is
hen I decided to write a book on negotiations.

How To Negotiate Like A Pro has won six book awards. It won the 2006 DIY Book
stival Price for best "How To Book" which honors independent and self-published
ooks on the cutting edge. It was also a Finalist in the ForeWord Magazine 2007
ook of the Year Awards and a Finalist in the Self-Help Category for the National
st Books 2007 Awards sponsored by USA Book News. It won two Runner-Up
vards from the New York Book Festival 2007 and an Honorable Mention from the
ondon Book Festival.

As I continued to mediate cases, mostly online, I also saw the same phenomenon
d I decided to write a sequel called *How To Mediate Like A Pro: 42 Rules for Medi-
ng Disputes.* In *How To Mediate Like A Pro,* I explain each rule of mediation and
ovide a script so that the readers can use the actual language in their own media-
ns if they like. My approach is pragmatic and practical since it is based on my own
perience dealing with real parties trying to resolve their disputes through media-
n.

How To Mediate Like A Pro will give you strategies and practical tips for the medi-
on process. It will give you insight on how to deal with difficult parties, how to
eak an impasse, and how to close the deal. It will show you how to talk like a medi-
or and how to mediate online and in the workplace. There are reference materials
 the Appendices, including a Glossary of terms, templates, and state and federal
ources. After you read this book, you should be able to *Mediate like a Pro..*

1

WHAT IS MEDIATION?

In mediation, the parties agree to work with a neutral third-party facilitator, the mediator, to resolve their dispute. The main difference between negotiations and mediation is that in negotiations, the parties work directly with each other, while in mediation the parties work with the mediator who facilitates the settlement.

Here are some of the characteristics of mediation.

- The parties agree to work with a facilitator or mediator to resolve a dispute.
- A mediator does not make a ruling like a judge or arbitrator.
- Mediation is voluntary so either party may choose to stop at any time.
- The mediator is imparital and does not represent either party's interests.
- A mediator may meet with both parties, a joint session, or individually with one party, a caucus. When meeting in caucus, what is said to the mediator is confidential unless the party agrees that the information can be shared.
- A mediator can be used when direct negotiations failed.
- A mediator can be used when the parties don't like each other.
- A mediator may be able to defuse conflicts or disagreements between the parties.
- The mediator may play devil's advocate or give a reality check to the parties.
- Mediation is not therapy.
- If the case cannot be resolved through mediation, the parties may try arbitration.

What Are The Differences Between Mediation and Negotiation?

Negotiation: The parties agree to work with each other to resolve a dispute.
Mediation: The parties agree to work with a mediator to resolve a dispute.

Negotiation: The parties always meet with each other.
Mediation: A mediator may meet with both parties jointly or meet individually with one party which is called a caucus.

Negotiation: The parties can bind themselves in an agreement.
Mediation: The mediator has no decision-making authority and cannot bind the parties. A mediator does not make a ruling like a judge or arbitrator.

Negotiation: The parties have their own interests in the negotiation.
Mediation: The mediator is neutral and impartial and does not represent either party's interests.

Negotiation: The parties use persuasion to get the other side to agree with them.
Mediation: The mediator may play devil's advocate or give a reality check to the parties, but it is not the mediator's role to persuade the parties.

Negotiation: Some negotiations fail because the parties won't talk to each other.
Mediation: A mediator may be used because the parties prefer a third party.

Negotiation: Some negotiations fail because the parties have too many conflicts.
Mediation: A mediator may be able to defuse conflicts or disagreements.

Negotiation: Some negotiations are not voluntary such as union negotiations.
Mediation: Mediation is voluntary and either party may choose to stop at any time.

Negotiation: When the parties can't agree, they reach a deadlock or impasse.
Mediation: When negotiations reach an impasse, the parties may try mediation.
Arbitration: When mediation reaches an impasse, the parties may try arbitration.

2

THE ROLES OF THE MEDIATOR

mediator plays many roles. A mediator is a facilitator who educates the parties and plains the process. He does what is necessary to help the parties reach an agreement. The mediator contacts the parties, sets up the meetings, and makes the arrangements for the mediation sessions. He also determines when the breaks and ucuses will be held, keeps track of each session, and follows up on loose ends. He n give a reality check to the parties' positions or tell the parties their expectations e too high. The mediator can also be the devil's advocate to expose the flaws in the rties' arguments. The mediator also works as a filter and takes what is said by one rty in caucus and rephrases it so it is not inflammatory. The mediator maintains utrality and makes sure that there is no bias or favoritism in the process.

ULE 1. THE MEDIATOR SETS THE TONE

ie mediator sets the tone for the mediation. My idea of a good mediator is someone .o is fair, honest, and creative. That is the tone I like to create. As in anything else, st impressions are very important. The mediator should look the part when he nes into the room. This means wearing professional clothes such as a suit. A man uld wear a jacket and tie. The mediator should act as though he knows what he is ing even if it is his first mediation. I always have a nice briefcase and a notebook. e mediator should give good eye contact and be a good listener. He should seem owledgeable yet approachable. The mediator should use a neutral tone of voice l never use sarcasm. I get right down to business and start with my opening statent which I use as a checklist for everything I want to say (See Appendix A.)

ript

job is to facilitate the mediation and to be fair, neutral, and creative.

RULE 2. LET THE PARTIES TELL THEIR STORY

Most parties need to tell their story to someone. Just telling their side of the story can be therapeutic. Some parties may feel ignored because no one has really listened to them. The mediator does not need to comment on the story as told by the parties. Usually telling the story is enough, but sometimes the parties need to vent their negative feelings and emotions to get them out of their system. Venting allows the parties to finally move forward. Other parties never stop venting and the mediator may have to step in so the mediation can move forward.

There are pros and cons as to whether both parties should be present during the venting process. The mediator will have to make that judgment call. By allowing both parties to hear the venting, it allows the other side to understand what the other party is going through. On the other hand, if it gets too emotional, it might not be helpful in resolving the mediation. Sometimes it is helpful to do the venting in a caucus so the other side does not witness it. Venting in caucus can allow the party to freely show the anger or frustration he feels toward the other party.

For example, a wife in a divorce case may be so intent on venting and documenting everything the husband has done wrong, that she is not even thinking about settling the mediation. She only wants to blame the husband. The mediator has to figure out a way to get beyond the emotions of the past to deal with the current issue of custody or visitation. The mediator needs to ask the other party what they want *now* to resolve the dispute. If one party cannot get beyond the venting phase, that may be a sign that the party may need therapy and that the case will never get resolved.

Script

If we are going to resolve this, we need to look to the future, not the past.
You need to get beyond the hurt you are feeling and look at the impact.
I know that this has been painful, but we need to discuss these issues.

RULE 3. THE MEDIATOR SETS GROUNDRULES

Groundrules help the mediator keep order. They set the boundaries for behavior in the mediation. If the parties are too emotional, they may lose control. If the parties lose control, the mediation is never going to be resolved. One way to prevent angry outbursts is to include groundrules in your opening statement at the first mediation session (See Rule 10.) Then it is understood that tantrums and outbursts will not be tolerated. If one side has an outburst, the mediator must nip it in the bud by calling

ucus and dealing individually with the offending party. If discourteous behavior is
ondoned, then the parties may not take the mediator seriously. One side may try to
ait the other party or even try to bait the mediator. The mediator must get the par-
es focused on the goals of the mediation.

cript

egotiations can get emotional, but you need to control your outbursts.
his is a violation of our groundrules and I am stopping the session for today.

ULE 4. THE MEDIATOR DOES NOT SHOW RUSTRATION OR EMOTION.

mediator should generally have a poker face so that the parties cannot tell whether
is happy, frustrated, or how he thinks the mediation is going. This might take
actice because it is human nature to show a little emotion when things are not
ing well. For example, if one party says something stupid, the mediator should not
ll his eyes. If the mediator finds a party's behavior annoying, it is important to keep
ese feelings to himself. Everything the mediator says can be misinterpreted by one
the parties. How something is said is almost as important as what is said. The
ediator cannot be patronizing or sarcastic to either side. The only time that emo-
n might be warranted is if the mediator is trying to make a point that will posi-
ely affect the progress of the mediation.

ript

m a neutral and my job is to keep the mediation on track.

ULE 5. MEDIATION IS NOT THERAPY; EDIATION IS NOT LEGAL ADVICE

diation is not the same as psychotherapy, counseling or legal advice. Mediation
not replace counseling. Generally a mediator should stop the mediation if he
ieves that one of the parties should see a therapist or mental health counselor.
n though many mediators may also be therapists or lawyers, a mediator cannot do
h. Even if a lawyer, a mediator cannot give legal advice. What he can do is tell the
ties that they may seek legal advice if he thinks that circumstances warrant it. In

addition, a mediator who is also a therapist cannot give counseling during the mediation.

What Are The Differences Between Mediation And Therapy?

Mediation: Mediation is results-oriented.
Therapy: Therapy is feelings-oriented.

Mediation: Mediation deals with solving problems.
Therapy: Therapy deals with pain, hurt, and changes in behavior.

Mediation: A trained therapist can be a trained mediator. A trained mediator cannot be a therapist and mediator at the same time.
Therapy: A trained mediator can be a trained therapist. A trained therapist cannot be a therapist and mediator at the same time.

Mediation: The mediator mostly resolves issues in the present and future.
Therapy: The therapist mostly looks to the past for resolving issues in the present.

3

NEUTRALITY, BIAS, AND ETHICS

he essence of a mediator's effectiveness is that he is neutral, ethical, and without ias. The mediator's reputation and integrity are of the utmost importance. This apter will give some rules for maintaining that neutrality.

RULE 6. THE MEDIATOR MUST BE NEUTRAL.

Iediators should be neutral in everything they do. For example, if a caucus lasts 30 inutes with one side, the caucus with the other side should be about 30 minutes, o. If a long caucus cannot be avoided, the mediator needs to explain that the other rty should not read anything into it. It is human nature to wonder why the media-r spent so much time with one side and so little time with the other.

Sometimes the other party thinks that the mediator is stating his opinion when e mediator is only restating the other side's opinion. Instead of asking, "Why was e item refurbished?" The mediator might say, "The buyer says that the item was furbished." Otherwise, the seller might think you are taking sides. Some parties are ore sensitive than others. Since many feel so strongly about their position, they are oking for an opportunity to show that the mediator is on the other person's side, o. Appearing neutral is the one of the most important things the mediator does. It lps instill confidence in the mediation process.

ript

a mediator, it is my obligation to be neutral.
lo not take sides.
lo not weigh the evidence.

RULE 7. THE MEDIATOR MUST NOT HAVE ANY BIAS.

Neutrality is more than just being fair and objective. The mediator must also have a lack of bias. We all know that we can't discriminate or treat someone differently on the basis of sex, race, color, age, religion, pregnancy, marital status, disability or national origin. Here are some practical suggestions on not showing bias or discrimination:

1. Don't treat men differently from women.

    A. Don't call women "dear," "sweetie," or "honey."

    B. Don't call women by their first name and men by their last name.

    C. If both a man and woman are doctors, don't call the woman "Mrs." and the man "Dr."

    D. Don't be flirtatious with either sex; it might be interpreted as sexual harassment.

2. Don't make sexist, racist, ethnic, or religious comments and don't let the parties make these kinds of comments, either.

    A. Women don't like to have women bosses.

    B. We hired a minority once; it did not work out.

    C. We are proud to have an Islamic Vice-President.

3. Avoid stereotypes such as the following:

    A. Men are better in math.

    B. Latins are always late.

    C. Older employees work more slowly.

RULE 8. THE MEDIATOR MUST KEEP HIS PERSONAL OPINIONS OUT OF THE MEDIATION

It is important that the mediator check his personal opinions at the door before trying to mediate anything. Ideally a mediator does not know anything about the dis ite and starts with a clean slate. Even if the mediator knows the parties, any econceptions must be avoided while mediating the dispute. Even if the parties are de, obnoxious, and insulting, the mediator can still help resolve the dispute though it may be more difficult.

The mediator cannot be swayed by the parties' opening statements. No matter w persuasive one side might be, I always say to myself, "there is more than one side any story." In mediation, it is really not important who is right and who is wrong. hat is important is how to resolve the dispute so both parties can walk away some- at satisfied. If one side asks me what I think or what my opinion is, I am very uctant to give it. I usually say it is not important what I think; it is only important at the other side thinks.

ript

is not important what I think. It is only important what the other side thinks. *y job is to facilitate.*

ULE 9. THE MEDIATOR MUST BE ETHICAL

mediator must be fair, honest, and ethical. Whether you are a professional media- , mediating at work, or mediating with your family, it is always important for the diator to keep his reputation intact. It is always better to err on the side of being ical and honest. If something has the appearance of being unethical, even though s technically not unethical, I don't do that either. I tell myself that once something pens to my reputation or credibility, it is very difficult, if almost impossible, to it back.

It is important not to discuss the mediation outside the mediation itself. The diator needs to be careful and not socialize or say anything that could be misinter- ted. I usually have lunch at a different place from the parties if feasible. If this is possible, I sit and read the newspaper in a corner. If I do happen to see one of the ties, I say something very neutral like, "How's it going?" I never make any refer- e to the case at hand. If the other side sees you talking with the other party, he y think you are talking about the case.

ipt

nnot discuss anything about the case now. Please ask me that question when are back in session.

4

OPENING STATEMENT

Rule 10. Give a Good Opening Statement

Before the mediation begins, the mediator makes an opening statement with both parties present. The opening statement is very important since it provides the framework for the mediation. It also gives the mediator an opportunity to explain the procedure and terms to the parties. This is particularly important if it is a party's first mediation. Even if the parties are very experienced, the opening statement should never be skipped. The opening statement establishes the role of the mediator and allows him to be in charge of the process. If done properly, the opening statement can instill confidence in the mediator and the process. It is also a good time to set expectations or groundrules. The mediator can explain the process and the definitions of key terms such as caucus, confidentiality, and ethics in his own words. The opening statement starts the process of cooperation and commitment to work together. It is also a way to set out the initial agenda. It is important for the mediator to have an opening statement checklist so all provisions are covered.

There are some provisions that a mediator is ethically bound to include in the Opening Statement. Be sure to check your state's rules to see if there are provisions you must include in the opening statement. For example, in Florida, a mediator is required to include the following: 1. Mediation is concensual (See C. What is Mediation?) 2. Mediator is impartial facilitator without authority to impose a resolution (See F. Neutrality, H. Ethics and I. Self-determination.) and 3. Communications made in a mediation are confidential unless required or permitted by law (See G. Confidentiality.)

Opening Statement Provisions

I. **Preliminaries:**

A. Introduction of Mediator: After introducing themselves, some mediators like to add their qualifications at this point. I like to make the opening statement about the parties and not about me. If specifically asked by the parties, I will give my certifications. and say the number of mediations or the different kinds of mediations I have mediated.

B. Introduction of parties

It is important to get the names and proper pronunciations of the parties so that you can address the parties properly. It could be embarrassing if you were mispronouncing a party's name. You will need the addresses and phone numbers for your records and to send your invoices to get paid if you are not paid at the mediation. Getting business cards can facilitate this process and I Like to staple small cards to the file so they don't get lost.

I don't always ask the parties how they want to be addressed. Some people don't feel comfortable using first names and others feel that Mr. or Mrs. is too formal. Don't call one party by their first name and another by their last name. It will appear that you are too familiar with the one you are calling by the first name. The other party may think you are being impartial. You will also want to determine if anyone is missing, or anyone is observing. Are there any witnesses or attorneys present?

C. What is Mediation?

Mediation is a way to resolve problems by mutually agreeing to use a third-party neutral or facilitator. The mediator helps the parties identify the issues, search for solutions, and facilitate voluntary agreements between the parties. The parties make the decisions not the mediator.

D. Mediation terms

Mediation has its own language and there over forty-five mediation terms in the glossary found in Appendix B. Many of these terms have special meanings that are different from common English usage.

Mediator's Responsibilities

What are Mediator's Roles?

The mediator is a facilitator who helps the parties resolve the dispute. He does not make a ruling like a judge or arbitrator. He does not give legal advice and he is not a therapist.

Neutrality of Mediator

The mediator does not represent either party and he does not take sides. He usually does not make a suggestion for a solution unless requested by both parties. The mediator has to be vigilant to make sure that both parties think he is impartial. For example, if I spend more time in a caucus with one party, I reassure the parties that I am not being impartial and that I had more questions.

G. Confidentiality
When the mediator meets individually with the parties in caucus, he will ask questions about the issues. These caucus discussions will be kept confidential. The mediator will not tell the other side anything said to him in caucus unless the party agrees that all or part the information can be divulged. For example, a party may tell the mediator he wants $100 but will take $80 for an item. The mediator would tell the other side you want $100 and would not say that you would be satisfied with $80. It is important that the mediator make this commitment to the parties that their information is confidential and that even when the mediation is over, he will not divulge anything about the mediation In Florida, communications made during the mediation are confidential except where disclosure is required or permitted by law. You may want to check your state rules on this. The mediator will ask the parties not to discuss the mediation with anyone, either. In some cases, there could be liability for the parties and the mediator if they do so.

H. Ethics
The mediator will pledge to conduct the mediation in an ethical manner. It is important that the mediator be fair, objective, and unbiased. He will only discuss the case in a mediation session and will only discuss the case with both parties present unless there is a scheduled caucus with one party. I ask the parties to let me know if they perceive something as unethical or impartial so we can discuss further.

III. Parties' Rights and Responsibilities

I. Self-Determination
Decisions made during the mediation are to be made by the parties not the mediator The job of the mediator is to facilitate. The mediator cannot coerce the parties or improperly influence the mediation. The mediator may think he has the perfect solution for the parties, but if he tries to impose that solution on the parties, he is going beyond the ethical bounds of the mediator's role. The mediator cannot insist that one party make a decision with which they are uncomfortable. In addition a mediator cannot misrepresent any factor or circumstance in conducting the mediation. If one party cannot maintain his self-determination, then the mediator should post

ne or close the mediation. The mediator can provide input and make suggestions
r alternatives, but the final decision is that of each party.

Voluntariness

ediation is voluntary and either side can decide to discontinue the mediation at any
ne. A mediator cannot be coercive or exert undue influence if one side wants to
p the mediation. That is the party's right. Of course, the mediator can discuss the
nsequences and other alternatives as long as he lets the party make the ultimate
cision.

Authority

is very important that both parties have binding authority to resolve the case and
: mediator needs to ask some questions to see if the parties do have authority. Oth-
vise, the mediation could be a waste of time. The mediator must determine at the
tset whether both parties have authority to resolve the case. If a party represents
nself, there is no problem. There can be a problem if, for example, someone from
insurance company has not been authorized to settle the case and must call in any
ers. Ask to see an agreement to see if the party is authorized to settle the dispute. If
ties do not have authority, adjourn the mediation until the parties get authoriza-
n. Otherwise the proceeding could be a waste of time if you find out at the conclu-
n that one party does not have the authority to settle.

. Mediation Mechanics

Caucusing

e mediator will meet with each party separately so that each party can speak freely
the mediator without the other party being present. This allows the parties to tell
mediator what their current position is and what their fallback positions are. This
ws the mediator to talk with the parties candidly without the other side being
sent. Caucusing can also save embarrassment if one party is not behaving properly
I the mediator can basically talk to him in private. The caucus is an important tool
nediation and much of the soul-searching goes on there.

Questions

e mediator will ask each party questions about the case so that he can better
lerstand the issues. I encourage the parties to let me know if they don't under-
d why I am asking the question. I also try to encourage the parties to ask about
proceedings. I also try to instill the concept that there is no stupid question and if
party has a question, the other party probably has the same question but is reluc-
t to ask it.

N. Impasse

The parties reach an impasse when they are deadlocked and no agreement can be reached. At that point the mediator has to try to help the parties get out of the dead lock. However, if that is not possible, I ask the parties whether they want me to offer a possible solution or whether they want me to close the case. I get a variety of answers on that. Some want to just give up and get on with their lives. Others will be willing to try some alternatives to see if there is a possibility of settlement with which both parties can live.

V. Procedural Issues

O. Groundrules

Here are some examples of groundrules or guidelines that I like to us. These can be modified to suit every mediation.

1. We will use common rules of courtesy. Only one person will speak at a time.
2. No one will use profanity.
3. Meetings will start on time.
4. Cellphones can only be used during breaks
5. Either party can request a caucus, but the mediator will make the final decision.
6. Both parties agree to comply with reasonable requests for information.
7. The party requesting the information agrees to pay reproduction costs.
8. The parties agree to discuss and confirm the date of their next mediation session at the close of every session.

P. Note-taking

I tell the parties that I will be taking notes through the mediation. I explain that if I am writing, that does not mean I am not listening. I explain that these notes help me keep track of where we are in the case. The notes are helpful to know where to start there are multiple sessions. I explain that these are my notes which I do not share with anyone and they are only taken to help me facilitate the case.

Q. Housekeeping issues

The housekeeping details are important to the parties especially if they are in a facility that is new to them. The parties want to know where the bathrooms and where to go when the other side is caucusing with the mediator. The parties need to know when breaks will generally be taken and when the lunch hour will be. The mediation will run more smoothly if everything is explained before the mediation begins. It also helps to agree on a finishing time, too. If the mediation is going well and parties need a little more time, these times can be extended. The parties need to know what the

ll phone policy is so that you don't have a cell phone ringing when it is not sup-
sed to be ringing.

Opening statements by parties in joint session
Both parties will make an opening statement.
Please include what you want in your opening statement.
I will ask for volunteers to go first. If no one volunteers or both volunteer, I will do
oin toss.

Rules for attorneys, if present
one or both parties are represented by attorneys, I implement the groundrule that
: parties will speak for themselves, not the attorneys. In addition, I tell the parties
it if they wish to speak with their attorneys before answering a question, they can
uest a private caucus with their attorney

ample of an opening statement is found in Appendix A.

5

HOW TO GET STARTED

Rule 11. Get the Parties To Say What They Want

Getting the parties to say what they want may seem obvious, but many parties real[ly] don't know what they want. Many are so angry that they have not even asked them selves how the issue can be resolved. They may want to hash and rehash the circum stances that got them into this mediation. By answering the mediator's question their goals can be clarified. In addition to knowing what they want, they also need [to] know what they are willing to give up in order to get what they want. Generally on[e] party can get what he wants if he is willing give up something for it.

How does the mediator find out what the parties want? Sometimes just asking th[e] other side what they want will give you some idea. This should usually be done i[n] caucus. However, the mediator may need to take the initial response with a grain [of] salt and ask for a backup position. Sometimes the parties don't realize that son[e] compromise is in order and that they will not get 100 % of what they want. Som[e] times one side wants something that is not important to the other. Ask the part[ies] what they are willing to trade to get what they want.

Script

The other party won't give you what you want unless he knows what that is.

Rule 12. Find Out If The Parties Want Something Other Than Money

Sometimes the other party wants something other than money such as time or apology. We are so used to mediating about money that sometimes we forget t[he] money is not everything. For example, a truly heartfelt apology can go a long way to resolve a dispute. If the other side feels that the apology is sincere, the apology may even be enough to close the deal. An employee might want time-off instead of money such as part-time work, flextime, or vacation time. Sometimes what is wanted is convenience rather than money. The mediator can help determine if there are non-monetary solutions to the dispute. One side may be willing to make concessions if there are no additional costs.

Sometimes the other side wants something that is not important to the other party. If the mediator can find out what that is, it can be a painless way of resolving a dispute. For example, an employee might want a raise and a new title. If the employer can agree on a title that reflects the person's duties, even if there is not enough money for a raise, the employee might still get something he wants. If the mediator can determine what is important to that party, the mediation might get resolved.

Script

Is there something other than money that you want?
Sometimes a heart-felt apology will resolve a dispute.

RULE 13. GET THE PARTIES TO AGREE ON THE ISSUES AND PRIORITIZE THEM

If both parties can agree on the issue or issues in the beginning, this saves time and effort. The mediator can work with each party, in caucus, to prioritize each side's issues. Then in a joint session, the mediator can help the parties agree on the issues to be discussed. If it is a fairly complex issue, it helps to put the issue or issues in writing.

Once the issues are known, the parties can decide the order for mediation. Some mediators like to start with the easy issues to gain some momentum and then move on to the more complicated items. Other mediators like to start with a complex issue so that when that gets resolved, the less important issues fall into place. If this is the mediator's first mediation, it is probably better to start with the easy items. This develops mutual trust and respect that can carry on through the rest of the mediation and help set the tone for the rest of the sessions. Starting with a complex issue can get the mediation bogged down so that the parties are frustrated and angry before any real work has begun.

Script

Let's agree on the smaller issues before we move on to the more complex ones. Once the difficult issue is resolved, it will be smooth sailing.

RULE 14. GET THE PARTIES TO DO THEIR RESEARCH

Once the parties know what they want, they must do their research and preparation. That could be as simple as listing the arguments on a sheet of paper or as complex as a study determining the amount of money actually needed for employees' salaries. Either way, the parties need to be prepared. The parties need to know the rationale behind their demands and a good estimate of their costs, including future costs. The mediator can ask questions in the caucus and point out flaws in the research. The mediator can also work on gaining some consensus about some of the numbers. If both parties can agree on the methodology, it will be easier to agree on the final outcome. If the parties don't have the research to back up their demands, the other side is unlikely to grant them their requests.

Script

I am a little confused at how you arrived at your numbers.
I would like to know the process and rationale you used.
If both parties can agree on the methodology, then it will be a lot easier to agree.

RULE 15. DON'T LET THE PARTIES GET BOGGED DOWN WITH PRINCIPLES

When someone says, "It's not the money, it's the principle," I know that the mediation is in trouble. That is because the party is making a judgment call that it is more important to be a martyr than to settle the case. Feeling that you are right can be a heady emotion, but it has no place in mediation. When someone is obsessed with the principle of a situation, that person is still emotionally vested in his feelings. Unless the mediator can help the parties get beyond those emotions, the dispute is not likely to be resolved.

However, this knowledge can be used to good advantage. Since one side has stated that money is not the issue, other strategies might work. The mediation may be

solved by one party giving an apology, changing procedures, or doing something
se that allows the other side to stay within their principles. I try to explain that fault
 not the essence of the mediation. It is not a question of who is right or who is
rong but how to resolve the situation. Some parties will never get beyond their
inciples and those cases will not be resolved.

cript

ow can we get beyond this blame game and move forward to a solution?
it important to you that the case get settled?
is not really important as to who is right or who is wrong.

ULE 16. DON'T LET THE PARTIES GET BOGGED OWN WITH THE FACTS

is absolutely essential to get beyond who is right and who is wrong and get to what
going to resolve the case. Sometimes one party will be obsessed with the facts of the
se and want to go through chapter and verse about everything that went wrong.
is party may have a chronology with dates and times and what was said by each
rty. He may relish reliving every terrible detail. The mediator can't let the parties
 bogged down by the facts. Going through every detail is counterproductive. The
ts need to be replaced with some solutions. The mediator may allow the party to
nt in caucus, but then the mediation needs to get back on track. If one side is only
erested in the facts, he usually won't want to compromise and chances are the situ-
on won't be resolved.

ript

's not get bogged down with all the details; let's look for solutions.
velling in the past can be counterproductive. Let's look at the present to see
at can resolve this case.

ULE 17. KEEP THE MOMENTUM AND TEMPO OING

e mediator should try to keep both the momentum and tempo going. If one party
ps saying "no" to all the proposals, the mediator needs to figure out why. Are
re other ways to give that side what it wants? Even a minor change, a compromise,

or a rephrasing might make it more palatable. If this is an important issue, perhaps a trade-off or package deal might work. The other side might be motivated by getting something they want.

The tempo of the mediation is very important. The mediator needs to know the parties' personality traits and know how to deal with them. If the mediator knows the preferred tempo of each side, he/she can use that information to help resolve the case. Some parties want to go over every little detail and don't care if the session lasts all day or night. Others want to only look at the big picture and want to spend as little time on the details as possible. The mediator must adjust the tempo accordingly. In addition, the mediator may need to spend more time in individual caucus with a detail-oriented party so the big picture person does not get bored or lose interest. There may be reasons, outside the mediation, that one party does not want to end the mediation. For example, an employee might not want to go back to his regular job and hopes to string out the mediation sessions as long as possible. The mediator needs to be aware all these factors and adjust the tempo and rhythm accordingly.

Script

Now that we have agreed on some major provisions, I think we can pick up the pace.
We may be going a little too fast.
Let's sleep on it and finish tomorrow.

6

ROLE OF THE CAUCUS

uring the caucus, the mediator can say things to one party confidentially that he
ould not say in a joint meeting. He can also give a reality check to the other party so
at his expectations won't be so high. Here are some rules that can be used in cau-
s.

ULE18. WHAT IF?

is an important strategy for the parties to have a backup plan. As they say, one
ould not put all one's eggs in one basket. The mediator can help the parties come
 with alternatives by asking the parties questions that start with *how* or *what if?*
hat if the other party rejects this? *How* can you sweeten the deal? *How* can you close
 deal? *What if* the other party rejects this? *What* is your backup plan? With the
propriate *what if* questions in caucus, the mediator can help each party come up
th some alternatives that will help seal the deal. Having a Plan B gets easier the
 re the parties mediate. The parties can learn to be more flexible and react to what
 other side wants.

ript

hat if the other party rejects this?
hat is your backup offer?

ULE 19. GIVE A REALITY CHECK

 dispute is to be resolved, the parties have to be realistic. Some parties start with
ally exaggerated proposals just so they can give up something later on. When one
ty asks for something outrageous or unreasonable, there has to be a reality check.
 s going to be up to the mediator, in most cases, to give that reality check. The

mediator might use his sense of humor to convey that what the party is asking for is totally out of the question or off the wall.

Whether it is a car, a house, or a coin on eBay, the parties need to know what it is worth before the mediation can be resolved. A good source of reality pricing is the internet, especially eBay. Looking at selling prices for comparable items can be a good reality check. What an item is worth is often a lot less than what was paid for it unless the item is extremely rare. It is important that the parties use the right comparables. For example, the value of a coin can be affected by the date, condition, mintage, and rarity. If the item is readily available, buyers might not offer much because they know they can easily get it somewhere else. However, if an item is rare, then the whole psychology is different. Now the buyer knows that if he doesn't buy it from you, there probably won't be another chance any time soon. The mediator can get the parties closer to settlement by showing them what the item is really worth.

A reality check does not have to relate to the value of an item. A reality check can involve any other issue in the dispute. For example, a party who believes his position is absolutely correct and that the other party should give him what he wants needs a reality check as to how mediation works. Some parties believe that the mediation settlement should be apportioned somehow with right and wrong. Some people wrongly believe that the mediator's job is to convince the other side to do what the "right side" wants. If one party's position is outrageous, the mediator can try to give a reality check and bring the party back to Earth. If the reality check does not work, then it may be time to question whether the mediation will ever be resolved.

Script

Have you checked the eBay prices for this item?
How rare is this item?
If you don't get a little more realistic, this case will never be resolved.

RULE 20. APOLOGIZE IF NECESSARY

Sometimes one party only wants an apology and the other side is too stubborn to give one. This is where the mediator can step in. One side can get very childish and say "he has to apologize first" or "I did not do anything wrong." If both sides believe this the mediator will have his work cut out for him. As a mediator, I try to explain that even if giving an apology is difficult, it can be phrased so it does not violate the party's "principles." I try to explain that even if one side believes the other side wrong, an apology might still resolve the dispute.

Why is an apology so important to some parties? It is a way to get their respect, dignity, and reputation back. An apology can be very satisfying to the other side if he feels he has been vindicated. I try to explain that an apology may be a cheap way to resolve a dispute. I focus on the goal of resolving the mediation so that the apology will not be that painful. I try to get the party to swallow his pride and just apologize. I also point out that a half-hearted apology or a sarcastic apology will make things worse. A good apology is when one party accepts blame and responsibility for his actions and shows some kind of remorse or regret. For some, an apology alone will resolve the conflict. For others, the apology is a condition that must be met before even discussing the substantive issues.

Script

If you want to settle this dispute, it is important that you apologize.
The other side wants you to accept responsibility and blame for what you did.

RULE 21. EVERYONE MAKES MISTAKES

Things happen and mistakes are inevitable. The mediator can help the parties deal with mistakes. There are two sides to a mistake: 1) the party who makes the mistake and 2) the party who is affected by the mistake. I try to explain to the party making the mistake that they need to "fess" up as soon as possible. It is better for the party to tell the other side about the mistake rather than for the other party to find out about it for himself. When a mistake is made, the other party usually assumes that it was done on purpose. I try to explain to a party who was affected by a mistake that this is a chance for him to be magnanimous and understanding. Many parties are totally unforgiving when mistakes are made and don't understand that mistakes are inevitable. The parties need to remember that the goal is to resolve the mediation. The sooner that the mistake is put behind them, the sooner the parties can concentrate on the solution. The solution to rectifying a mistake should not be overly complicated. For example, if the wrong item was sent to the wrong person, don't expect that party to send it to a third party. It might be better to offer a refund at this point. A lot of wasted effort can be directed at the events that led up to the mistake. The mediator's role is to concentrate on a solution and not on who made the mistake.

Script

We all make mistakes and let's see how we can move forward to resolve this.
Let's not dwell on who made the mistake; let's concentrate on correcting it.

RULE 22. BE A DEVIL'S ADVOCATE

Being a devil's advocate is a great way to give a reality check to one side. It helps the mediator point out the flaws in a side's arguments or proposals. When the mediator plays the devil's advocate, he is not being his own advocate. It is a convention so that it does not appear that the mediator is actually making the comments on his own behalf. By taking on the devil's role, the mediator can point out the flaws in the arguments. The other side cannot take offense since it is not the mediator talking but the devil. This allows the party to get a reality check and hopefully change his position.

Script

Let me play devil's advocate for a minute. You are asking him to agree to something that is three times what he is paying now.

RULE 23. WATCH BODY LANGUAGE

Watching the parties' body language can help the mediator know more about the parties. If someone is avoiding eye contact, he or she might be lying. If a person's head is in their hand, he might be frustrated or tired. Stroking one's face usually means a person is thinking or planning the next move. If the other side is friendly that usually means confidence. If the other side is indifferent or hesitates, it could be a sign of weakness. A bead of sweat on the forehead might mean the party is nervous or agitated or that the room is hot. However, it is importance not to put too much stock into body language. Mediation is a lot like playing poker and there is a lot of bluffing going on. The other side might be trying to throw you off by his body language. Remember, the other side is probably looking at you to determine your state of mind. If you have had previous dealings with the parties, it might be easier to read the body language.

Script

Looking at body language is only a tool, so be careful how you interpret it.

7

HOW TO DEAL WITH DIFFICULT PARTIES

ιe mediator has to deal with many different kinds of personalities. When the par-
s are thoughtful, helpful and accommodating, the case usually gets resolved. How-
ɛr, when the parties are angry, greedy and vindictive, the mediation becomes much
ɔre difficult. Here are some of the personality types and what they say.

ɪgry Type: "This mediation is a joke." Generally this party is mad at the other
ɾty and the mediator and does not respect the process and does not trust the medi-
ɔr. He will do anything to disrupt the mediation process, including temper tan-
ms to try to undermine the mediator's authority.

ɪffing Type: "If I don't get what I want, I will walk away." This party may not
ɪderstand the consequences of making a threat that he does not keep.

ɪdictive Type: "The other side was wrong and I want him to pay." The party feels
t his side is the right one and will do anything to hurt the other side financially.
˙ example for a $50 case, he would want $500 for the aggravation and time spent
it at his hourly rate.

ɪversionary Type: "Let the games begin." The party may not care if the case gets
ɔlved because he is in it for the fun of the process. Whatever is offered, he will
ɪe back with new things to ask for because he is never going to be satisfied. It is
˙ thrill of the hunt, not the final outcome that is satisfying to him.

ɛedy Type: "This is what I want. Take it or leave it." The greedy type does not
ɪderstand how mediation works and that compromise is part of the process. The
ɛdy type feels that its position is correct and there is no point arguing the merits of
ɪr position.

Suspicious Type: "You are out to get me". I had a party take issue with the fact that I signed an email in an online mediation with MEdiator. He felt I was mocking him somehow by capitalizing the E. I tried to explain that it was a typo caused by fast typing and the second letter got capitalized, too. He also felt that I was also the seller masquerading as the mediator. Once the paranoia takes hold, it is difficult for the party to come back to reality. It seems that anything the mediator says is going to be misinterpreted.

Self-Righteous Type: "You decide who is right and who is wrong." This type feels that "right and principle" are on his side and, therefore, he wants the mediator to validate his position and agree that he is "right."

Here are some rules to use when dealing with difficult parties.

RULE 24. DON'T ALLOW TEMPER TANTRUMS

A party might have a temper tantrum to challenge the mediator's authority, especially at the beginning of the mediation. It is important for the mediator to take control of the mediation and nip such behavior in the bud. At the first sign of anger, discourtesy, or sarcasm, the mediator must take action. The party exhibiting such behavior is letting the mediator know he has no respect for the process or the mediator. This is totally unacceptable. The mediator might want to discuss this behavior with the party in a caucus session so as to save face and embarrassment. This allows the mediation to continue normally if the party does settle down. The party must be told that there are consequences of such behavior and, if it continues, the mediation will be terminated. If the mediator does make such a threat or consequence, he should always go through with it. Some parties like to test the mediator to see what he will do. Other parties like to stir the pot and put something in motion and see what happens. If the mediator decides that the party is truly not interested in mediating, it is his decision to terminate the mediation.

Script

That kind of outburst is unacceptable.
If it happens again, I am closing the mediation.

RULE 25. EXPLAIN THE REPERCUSSIONS OF WALKING AWAY

One party might feel that if he does not get what he wants, he is ready to walk away. For example, a party might decide that if he does not get the raise he is requesting that he is prepared to quit. The mediator can remind the party that there are other ways to mediate which don't have such dire consequences. On the other hand, the party may be testing the waters to see if he can get a pay increase in his current job.

If someone threatened to quit when I was a director of human resources, I would give him a piece of paper and ask him to write, "I resign," and sign and date it before he changed his mind. Of course, if I wanted to keep the employee, I would try to work something out. This is an extreme tactic and should only be used if an employee is really ready to walk. As a mediator, I advise parties not to bluff unless they are prepared to take the consequences. Don't say you are going to walk away if you are not willing to follow through. An employee will lose any negotiating power he had if he comes back the next day begging for his job back.

Script

If your employer must choose between giving you a promotion and you quitting, he might ask for your resignation.
Why don't you state all the reason you deserve a raise?
Don't threaten to quit unless you mean it.

RULE 26. DON'T ALLOW PARTIES TO OVERREACH

If one side uses ruthless tactics in a mediation, the other side will want to retaliate at the next mediation or even sooner. One side may have won the battle but will still lose the war. One side may have gotten major concessions, but the relationship may be deteriorated and full of distrust. Each side should try to get as much as they can in a mediation, but there will be consequences if one side goes too far. The consequences of overreaching might not be immediately apparent, but the other side will wait for the right moment to avenge their humiliation. The side who has overreached might not want to wait for retaliation and go ahead and meet with the other side and repair some of the damage. It is difficult to have a good working relationship after the mediation has gone sour. When mediating with a party on a regular basis, be careful not to overreach. Like an elephant, a losing party will never forget and will try to retaliate at the next opportunity.

Script

We don't trust you anymore.
I thought the mediation was going well until we were ambushed.
You went too far and took advantage of us.

RULE 27. DON'T ALLOW PARTIES TO CREATE DIVERSIONS

In the military setting, a diversion is created by releasing smoke to mask the location of moving troops. In the mediation setting, a diversion is a way to mask a side's true intention of what is important. A smoke screen is a diversionary tactic to take attention away from the main objective and give attention to something of little or no importance. This can backfire if the other side realizes what is happening. A decoy or red herring is a tactic to mislead the other party and create a diversion. Of course, the origin of the decoy is duck hunting, but the origin of the term red herring is more obscure. Red herring was rubbed on hounds to protect the hunted fox or fugitives from being caught. The hounds will smell the herring rather than the scent of the fox or men. A red herring is essentially a false clue or phony issue that is used to distract the voters or negotiators from the real issues. It is up to the mediator to make sure the parties don't create diversions.

Script

We know that the issue of seniority is just a smoke screen.
All that discussion was just a red herring. I know what the real issue is.

RULE 28. EXPLAIN THE REPERCUSSIONS OF THE TAKE IT OR LEAVE IT APPROACH

The take it or leave it approach was used in a famous labor case in the 1950's that involved Lemuel Boulware, a vice-president for General Electric. Mr. Boulware stated what the company could afford and presented his only offer as a package deal to the electrical union. Basically Mr. Boulware said, "take it or leave it." The Court determined that this was not good faith bargaining because there was no involvement

y the union. This take it or leave it approach is now called Boulwareism (sometimes
elled Boulwarism), named after that General Electric vice-president who first used

This one-sided approach should not be used in mediation. One side is saying this
what we want and basically refuses to discuss any alternatives. Some parties try to
ke over the mediator's role by using the take it or leave it approach. Instead of relin-
uishing control to the mediator, they tell the mediator exactly what they want and if
e other party does not agree, they want the case closed. Usually the other side is not
ing to agree to such a one-sided demand and an impasse is reached almost before
e mediation begins. When this happens, I will caucus with the party to see if there
any leeway. I explain that the essence of the mediation process is give and take. If
e party still does not want to deviate from his all or nothing approach or consider a
unter-offer from the other side, I will close the case.

cript

take it or leave it approach has no place in mediation.
n all or nothing approach does not allow both parties to participate.

ULE 29. YOU CAN MEDIATE WITH A LUNATIC

en if one side is totally unreasonable, it is still possible for the parties to resolve the
spute. As a mediator I usually don't tell a person how ridiculous his claim or
unter-offer is because he will probably be offended. I do try to point out what the
her side is willing to pay and ask if there is anything else he wants such as an apol-
y. Sometimes I use humor to try to deflect the party's frustration, but this can
metimes backfire and make him even madder. If the person insists on his outra-
ous position, the parties will probably reach an impasse or deadlock. If it seems
rly obvious that the party is playing a game and has no intent of resolving the dis-
te, I will try to get him to discuss it logically. These are the hardest cases to resolve
cause the other person often prefers to rant and rave rather than to work on settling
e real issues. If one party continues to be totally unreasonable, then I will close the
e.

ript

m trying to understand what you really want.
hink you are joking, right? Tell me what you really want.

RULE 30. A MEDIATOR DOES NOT MAKE DECISIONS

Sometimes one party wants the mediator to make a decision as to who is right or wrong like a judge or arbitrator. Of course, that party usually thinks he is right and that all the evidence shows that he should "win." He wants the mediator to validate his position. I have already explained the mediator's role in my opening statement, but I still get these requests. I point out that mediation is not the same as arbitration or court and that the mediator does not weigh the evidence and make a decision. The mediator is a facilitator not a judge. It is up to the parties to agree to a resolution not the mediator. It is hard for some parties to wrap their minds around the self-determination aspect of mediation. Sometimes they still want to know what the mediator thinks about the case and who is right or wrong. However, if both parties want me to make a recommendation, I will, but I won't make any determinations as to who is right or wrong. I try to switch the focus from fault to the issues. That is the only way the case will get resolved.

Script

I am a mediator not an arbitrator or a judge.
I do not make a decision or weigh the evidence.
If both sides agree, I will make a suggestion.

8

HOW TO CLOSE THE DEAL

n impasse occurs when the parties cannot reach agreement and are deadlocked. ere are some rules to chip away at the deadlock and close the deal.

RULE 31. TELL THE PARTIES WHAT WILL HAPPEN IF NO AGREEMENT.

emind the parties what will happen if there is no agreement and the mediation falls art. The parties will have to start all over again if the mediation breaks down, sulting in a loss of time, money, and energy. Anything that has already been agreed will not go into effect. I like to point out that in mediation, the parties can be the aster of their own destiny. If they go to court or to arbitration, they will lose the ntrol to fashion their own settlement. In addition, if a third party makes the deci- on, the parties might not like the result. As they say, it is the difference between the vil you know and the devil you don't know. Sometimes pointing out what will ppen if the parties cannot break the deadlock is enough to get the parties talking ain.

ript

the mediation fails, it will take the decision out of your hands.
the mediation is closed, neither party will get what it wants.
e if you can put your differences aside and work out some kind of compromise.

RULE 32. TAKE A BREAK

oth parties are clearly frustrated and tired, it might be time for a break. Clearing air and getting a fresh start can give a jump start to the mediation. It is important to try some new techniques since the old way of thinking has not worked. The mediator can give specific assignments to work on during the break and brainstorm with the parties when they get back to see if anything has been overlooked. This is the time to emphasize mutual interests that can help close the deal. This is also a good time to caucus with each party to see if there is anything else that can be offered. The mediator will try to find out if anything can break the deadlock. A break allows the parties to look at the issues with fresh eyes. If they are close to settlement, they may be motivated to break the deadlock rather than close the case and be in the same position they were before the mediation started.

Script

Let's take a break until tomorrow so we can look at this with fresh eyes.
Have you overlooked anything?

RULE 33. AGREE IN PRINCIPLE AND WORK OUT THE DETAILS LATER.

Sometimes the parties can agree on the principle of an idea and work out the details later. It is often easier to agree in principle rather than getting bogged down with working out every word and every possible contingency. Dotting the i's and crossing the t's can get very tiring and frustrating when there is an impasse. Agreeing in principle can be a morale booster and a shift in thinking can take place. This approach also can buy time. If there are other issues to work on, the actual language can be worked out at a later time. One party could write a draft and bring it to a later session. When both parties have already agreed in principle, it is a lot easier to work out the details.

Script

Let's agree in principle and work it out later.
We can work on other issues and flesh this out later.

RULE 34. TRY A TRADE-OFF OR PACKAGE DEAL

A tradeoff is sometimes called a *Quid Pro Quo*, which is Latin for *this for that*. If you give me this, I will give you that. It sounds fair and it is a way to compromise because both parties are getting something back in return. The parties need to determine

hat they want and what they are willing to give up. Many parties are more inter-
ted in what they are getting rather than what they are giving up. The mediator can
lp the parties fashion a trade-off that will be beneficial to both parties. Even if there
e other issues, a trade-off will help increase the momentum to resolve the other
ues. The mediator can also help with a package deal that will resolve all the remain-
g issues in the mediation. A deadline on the package deal usually hurries things
ng, too.

ript

you give me this, I will give you that.
ere is a package deal that will resolve all issues.

ULE 35. SPLIT THE DIFFERENCE.

litting the difference is a good strategy to use when parties are deadlocked. Split-
g the difference works well when the dollar amount is very close. The parties may
en be willing to accept something they might have rejected earlier in the mediation.
r example, the seller offers $500 and the buyer wants $400. Splitting the difference
$450 may seem like a good compromise. Splitting the difference can work if there
some momentum and the parties are willing to compromise to close the deal.

ript

hy don't we split the difference and call it a day?

ULE 36. THE DEVIL IS IN THE DETAILS

the excitement of resolving a long and complex dispute, it is tempting to stop the
diation when there seems to be initial agreement and put off writing down the
ails. I recommend that the parties work out as many details as they can while it is
fresh in their minds. It is amazing how fuzzy the recollection of complicated
ails can be after only a few days. Even when there is preliminary agreement, one
e wants may want an answer for every possible contingency. The mediator needs
anticipate these contingencies
As a mediator, you may feel that one person is being a real stickler. Even if one
ty insists on some detail that the other side feels is superfluous, the other party
y want to humor the other side and give in if it closes the deal. Of course, it is bet-
to have any loose ends cleared up now rather than later, but sometimes this is not

practical. Sometimes the parties have to agree in "principle" and leave the details to another day.

Script

Why spend a lot of time on something that probably will never happen?
If it is that important to you, let's include it.

RULE 37. GET THE PARTIES TO GIVE ONE MORE THING

Some parties in mediation are never going to be completely satisfied and always want the last word. Just when it looks as though the parties have agreed to all the issues and the case seems to be resolved, one of the parties wants one more thing. This is human nature, I guess, to squeeze as much out of the other side as possible. This extra bonus or gift is sometimes called a *Lagniappe*, which is a little gift a shopkeeper might add to a purchase in Louisiana. The word is derived from the Creole dialect of New Orleans and has a French spelling. Of course, asking for something else at the end of a deal can backfire. The other side may be so offended that something new is brought up at such a late time that the mediation never gets resolved. When the other side is frustrated because of the party's last ditch effort to get something more, I try to explain that this is also an opportunity to *get* one last thing.

Script

If the other side wants something else, you can get something else, too.

RULE 38. SHOW PARTIES THE BIG PICTURE

During mediation, we are always looking at the small picture. We are dealing with the facts and details of a dispute that is important to the parties, but it is generally not earth-shattering to anyone else. It is important to step back once in a while and see where the dispute is in the big picture of one's life, world events, etc. Some people have a lot of anger and frustration vested in the outcome of the mediation. When weighed against world peace or other important events, the mediation loses its significance. Sometimes looking at the big pictures reminds the parties to take themselves less seriously. Putting the mediation in perspective sometimes allows the parties to throw in the towel and close the mediation or give it one last try.

ript

won't be the end of the world if we don't resolve this.

't's try one more time to resolve this and if we can't, let's call it quits.

ULE **39.** KNOW WHEN TO HOLD AND WHEN 'O FOLD

st as the song says, you need to know when to close and when to fold. Some things ll never be resolved. However, if the parties are still making some progress, even at nail's pace, it might be worthwhile to keep plodding away. On the other hand, if : mediator has made several suggestions which were not met with any discussion or erest, this may be a sign that the impasse won't be broken. If the parties are very se in their proposals, there may be some hope. However, if the parties are still far rt, it may be time to look at closing the case. There are some cases that just won't settled and there is no point in wasting time and energy on a lost cause.

ript

nestly I don't know if they have any more to give.

u are so far apart in your positions that I suggest we close the case.

ne cases don't get settled and I think this is one of them.

ULE **40.** MEDIATION FOLLOW-UP

s not over when the mediation is finished. It is only over when there is a signed eement. It is very important for the parties to spend the time to look very closely he finished product and compare it to notes and drafts to see that everything is as ed. Even though both parties have agreed, sometimes the parties have a different lerstanding after the agreement is reduced to writing. In addition, it is important ook for misspellings and typos. A misplaced comma or period could change the ning of a whole section. It is human nature to want everything to be completed hurry. However, this final review is of utmost important and is the one thing that lld not be rushed.

The signed document needs to be reviewed to see if there is any follow-up lired. Once the agreement is approved, the mediator generally has no further con- with the parties. The mediator can explain to the parties the contingencies and deadlines that need to happen in the future. It will be up to the parties themselves to do follow-up.

Script

Is follow-up needed during the term of the agreement?
Make sure that there are no typos or mistakes.
Does this document accurately reflect the agreement?

RULE 41. THE MEDIATOR SHOULD NOT EXPECT THANKS OR GRATITUDE.

After the mediation is finished, the mediator should not expect thanks or gratitude. He needs to move on and go to his next case. The parties have short memories so don't expect any thanks for your hard work. The fact that the case has been resolved should be the only encouragement the mediator needs. Sometimes there is a mental letdown because the mediator has emotionally invested a lot of energy in the dispute. However, when it is over, it is over. Let it go. Even though the mediator should not expect thanks or gratitude, he can still thank the parties for their efforts.

Script

I really appreciate the time and effort you spent to resolve this dispute. Thanks.

RULE 42. GIVE YOURSELF A DEBRIEFING

The mediator should do a debriefing after each case. The debriefing is a way to evaluate the case and make changes in future mediations. It is a good chance to analyze what worked and what might need improvement. The answers to these questions will prepare you for the next mediation.

Script

Were any mistakes made?
What worked and why?
What could I have done differently?

9

HOW TO TALK LIKE A MEDIATOR

One of the hardest jobs of a mediator is to give a good response to the parties' concerns. After mediating thousands of cases, I have heard a lot of questions and concerns from the parties. The mediator has to give a response that informs without alienating one or both parties. Here are some responses that a mediator can make. They are not the only response but what I consider a good response.

Comments Made to the Mediator

Righteous Party: Just decide who is right or wrong.
Mediator's Response: That is not how mediation works. A mediator cannot decide who is right or who is wrong. In mediation, the parties decide what is right for them and how they will resolve the case. I only work as a facilitator and I do not weigh the evidence and determine who should win.

Suspicious Party: You are taking his side.
Mediator's response: I am by definition a neutral third party. Sometimes I play the devil's advocate and give the parties a reality check or suggest different alternatives. However, that does not mean I am taking sides.

Uncertain Party: What would you do?
Mediator's Response: Generally I don't like to give my opinion because it is really the other party's opinion that counts, not mine. However, since you asked me, I would give the other side the benefit of the doubt.

Impatient Party: This is taking too long and is a waste of time.
Mediator's Response: I know you think this is taking too long, but we are following process. Sometimes this can take time, but it cannot be hurried.

Unsatisfied Party: You don't know what you are doing! Where were you trained?
Mediator's Response: I am doing my best and I am always open to suggestions. I am not sure why you are asking the question, but I am certified by the Florida Supreme Court in County Mediation and have conducted over 7000 mediatons. Not all mediations are going to be successful. It often depends on whether both parties are willing to work on finding a solution.

Annoyed Party: You don't understand.
Mediator's Response: Maybe I don't understand. Can you try one more time to explain your position? Maybe I am missing something.

Party wants to quit: I don't want to continue the mediation.
Mediator's response: Mediation is by definition a voluntary process and you can decide to discontinue the mediation at any time. Do you want me try one more time to see if we can resolve this or do you want me to close the case now?

B. Comments About The Other Party

Principled Party: It is not about the money but the principle.
Mediator's Response: I understand that you believe you are right and you don't want to go against your principles. As a mediator, I do not determine who is right or wrong. It is possible to resolve a dispute without making that judgment call. What is it that you truly want? Is it an apology or a change in policy?

Take It or Leave It Party: This is what I want and I am not budging.
Mediator's Response: I understand you don't want to budge from your position. Unfortunately, the other side is not budging, either, and we are at an impasse. Mediation is a give and take and there has to be some compromise if the case is going to be resolved. If the impasse cannot be broken by one of the parties, then I will have to close the mediation. Why don't you split the difference and both parties get something?

Self-Righteous Party: Why should I apologize? He is the one who is wrong.
Mediator's Response: Sometimes an apology is an easy and cheap way to resolve dispute. Just because you apologize does not mean that you are taking anything away from your position. You can honestly say that you are sorry for the confusion or misunderstanding. An apology can go a long way to help the other party feel good about the situation. However, an apology must be sincere or it will make things worse.

Self-Righteous Party: I have done nothing wrong.

Mediator's Response: I don't like to think in terms of who is right or who is wrong. That is not the way to get something resolved. Let's look at some solutions that could resolve this situation.

Self-Righteous Party: He made the mistake. Why should I suffer?
Mediator's Response: Mistakes do happen. To err is human. I don't think he did it on purpose. This gives you a chance to be magnanimous and understanding.

Judgmental Party: It is not fair that I give something up.
Mediator's Response: Mediation is not about fairness or getting even. Both parties have to be willing to compromise to find a solution.

Disinterested Party: I don't care if this gets resolved. It is his problem.
Mediator's Response: The other side is motivated to resolve this situation. Can you think of anything the seller could say or do that might change your mind?

Angry Party: He makes me so mad.
Mediator's Response: I know you are upset. However, mediation is not going to be successful if the parties let their emotions interfere with resolving the dispute. Let's concentrate on what you want to settle this dispute. Do you want an apology?

Judgmental Party: The other side lied.
Mediator's Response: I know there is a misunderstanding between the parties. Whether he did it intentionally, I have no way of knowing. I suggest we give him the benefit of the doubt and let's move forward.

Disappointed Party: She does not know how to communicate.
Mediator's Response: I know that you did not receive any emails from her. Is it possible your spam filter blocked her emails. What do you want to tell her now? Let's move forward and see if we can communicate.

Defensive Party: Yes, I did make a mistake, but she overreacted
Mediator's Response: I am glad you admitted your mistake. Maybe she did overreact, but she was very upset. Would you be willing to apologize to her? Sometimes an apology can go a long way to help start some dialogue.

Defensive Party: She is making a mountain out of a mole hill.

Mediator's Response: I know you think that she is making too much out of this. However, this is very important to her and she can't help how she feels. Try to put yourself in her shoes. Is there any way you can make her an offer?

Unforgiving Party: I want others to see his feedback. I don't want to withdraw it.
Mediator's Response: I understand what you are saying and it is your choice. However, you are missing out on an opportunity to have your feedback withdrawn, too. If you don't care if your feedback remains as well, then I will close the case.

C. How the Mediator Can Reframe One Party's Position.

The mediator can change the tone of what is said to him. One side might be angry, distraught, and accusatory and say things that would solicit a negative response. Here are some examples of toning down the language.

Party: I am mad as hell and won't take it anymore!
Mediator's Interpretation: The other side is a little upset.

Party: He is a crook and liar.
Mediator's Interpretation. The other side does not believe you.

Party: He did not send the item.
Mediator's Interpretation: The party did not receive the item. Have you sent it yet?

Party: I want to quit this mediation.
Mediator's Interpretation: The buyer wants me to close the case.

Party: The other party is the biggest jerk I have ever met.
Mediator's Interpretation: The other party does not like what you have done.

Party: The item was smelly and filthy.
Mediator's Interpretation: The buyer says the item was not clean and had an odor.

Party: I don't trust him.
Mediator's Interpretation: He does not think you will do what you say you will.

Party: The seller ripped me off.
Mediator's Interpretation: The buyer says he does not like what you did.

Party: He is just stupid.

Mediator's Interpretation: He does not think you understand his position.

Party: Refurbished is supposed to be like new. This was a piece of garbage with scratches and dings.

Mediator's Interpretation: His idea of refurbished is different from yours. He says there were scratches and dings.

Party: I would not sell my house to him if he was the last person on earth.

Mediator's Interpretation: He has decided not to sell the house to you.

10

HOW TO MEDIATE ONLINE

With the advent of the internet, there will be more and more mediation on-line. You may be involved in a formal process with special software or a more informal type of mediation where the parties communicate by regular email. Mediating online has some fundamental differences from mediating in person. The major difference is that online mediation is not done extemporaneously; it is a time-delayed process. The mediator sends a message to both parties and then waits for a response. Since the mediator cannot see the person and cannot hear the person, all the cues are from the online message. You may guess the sex of the party by the name, but you really don't know the race, nationality, or other identifying factors. This anonymity is hard to get used to in the beginning, but in a way it is freeing not knowing anything about the parties except what they have told you about the dispute.

Since many Mediations online are going to be on eBay or other online auctions, have included a description of eBay.

What is EBay?

Ebay is an online auction where sellers can sell their items to willing buyers. It uses an automatic bidding system so that a buyer can enter the maximum amount he/she willing to pay and this information is kept confidential and not divulged to buyers or sellers. The eBay system compares your bids to any other bids on the item and, in effect, the system places bids by proxy on your behalf. It uses only as much of your bid as is needed to be the highest bidder. If another bidder has a higher amount, then you have been outbid and you will be notified so that you have the opportunity to make a higher bid.

EBay has revolutionized how people buy and sell antiques, collectibles and even new items. EBay does not handle the item; it only provides the online framework bid and charges insertion fees and a percentage commission of the final bid. EBay has its own rules and if you are not familiar with eBay or are a *newbie* (new to eBay), you may want to browse their website at http://www.ebay.com/. You can buy a pen em or a $100,000 car, but the concepts are basically the same regardless of the value f the item.

Here is an example of how it works. You see a gold coin and you bid $300. The urrent bid is $50. If someone else has already secretly bid over $300, then you will et a message that you have been outbid. If the highest secret bid on the coin was 200, your bid will be shown at the next increment or $205.00. If no one else bids efore the auction's deadline, then you will get the item for the $205, not your max-num bid of $300.

What is eBay feedback?

eedback is a way to evaluate a member's reputation and is the backbone of the eBay rocess. For each eBay transaction, the buyer and seller are allowed to rate each other y leaving a rating of positive, neutral, or negative. A positive gets a 1, a neutral gets a and a negative gets a minus 1. A glance at an eBay member's profile shows the total each of the three categories and the total percentage of positives. Of course, 100 % the best percentage, but if some one has 98 or 99 %, you know that there were only very few unsatisfied customers. If the negative feedback happened a long time ago, at is a positive sign. It is not unusual for a newbie to get a negative feedback when arning the ropes of eBay culture. However, if there are several recent negative feed-acks, that is a warning not to bid on their items. If a buyer likes the item and decides bid anyway, he cannot say he was not warned that things could go awry. EBay ers are very proud of feedback and can become very upset if someone gives them a gative rating especially if they think it is unjustified. If someone had a perfect rat-g of 100% before getting a negative feedback, that individual may go to great ngths to have that feedback withdrawn to get back their perfect score.

How can negative feedback be withdrawn?

both parties agree that feedback should be withdrawn, there is a mechanism rough eBay to withdraw the feedback. See the Ebay website www.ebay.com. Often the heat of the moment, a party may say something that they are willing to with-aw after their anger subsides. Feedback is no longer *removed;* it is only *withdrawn* nless the feedback contains objectionable language such as lewdness or profanity, nich will be removed directly by eBay.) Withdrawing feedback means that the neg-ve rating is removed for that one eBay transaction, but that people can still read feedback. If the parties cannot resolve their dispute themselves, then they can file ase with a mediation service for eBay buyers and sellers. For a small fee, a trained ediator will work with both parties online The mediator will send them joint and parate emails in an automated format and work as a facilitator to resolve their eBay dispute. If their feedback has not been withdrawn by eBay, the feedback can be withdrawn through the mediation process.

Here are some of the rules to use on online mediations:

A. Use Proper Online Etiquette

Certain rules of etiquette have evolved online. There are simple rules of courtesy that apply to email messages. Don't use expressions like lol (laughing out loud), brb (be right back), smiley faces, funny noises, colored texts, or anything else that might be distracting and unprofessional. Do not use all capital letters. This is like shouting and is considered very rude. It also is harder to read caps than lower case. Don't send large attachments via email that will take a long time to download. Don't write long messages; be short and sweet in your emails. Somehow the bald language accentuates the meaning of the language. Without the outside cues, online messages can sound cold and clinical. A joke or a funny remark may go flat because the other party does not hear the inflection you would use if you were saying the joke in person. The other side might not even get it and be insulted.

B. Be Careful of Your Typos and Misspellings

If your English is not proper, it can distract from your message. Because you are typing and thinking at the same time, it is easy to make mistakes which only get noticed after you have already sent the message. Use spell checker and grammar checker. However, this is not fail-proof because the spell checker will not flag a word if it is a word even though it might not be the word you intended. If you have read some of your emails after the fact, you know that it is easy to make typing mistakes and they are not easily spotted when you do your first proofread.

Everyone needs an editor. In a complex mediation, it is a good idea to put away your initial email and review it the next day for errors before sending it out. Once you have sent it, it is too late. You can create more problems if you are dealing with damage control with an email full of mistakes and typos. The parties can also be offended if the email looks carelessly written because of all the grammar and spelling errors. It sets a tone that you don't care and you are not professional. The parties also have a chance to study what you have written. In a face to face mediation, the other side can easily forget what was said, but in an online mediation, either party can go back and look at the emails and see exactly what was said.

Don't Send A Message Immediately After You Have Written It.

Mediating online is much more exacting than mediating in person. It is important not to act hastily after receiving a message especially if you are angry about something the side said. You may be tempted to send back a sarcastic or angry email. Remember that you are the mediator and you are supposed to be neutral and not have emotions. I write out what I want to say, but I don't send it out until the next day. Then look at it the next day and, in most cases, I often delete the whole thing or at least tone it down. I am usually somewhat relieved that I did not send the message in haste the day before.

The Mediator must have a thick skin

I am surprised at the mean things that the parties are willing to say to a mediator online. The parties are much bolder online than if they saw me face-to-face. Somehow the internet frees up their inhibitions. When I first started mediating, I was a little hurt and insulted by some of the comments such as, "You are not doing your job!" or "What a waste of money!" I wanted to send back a sarcastic comment right away. I had to give myself some of my own advice and wait until the next day to send my response. I had to remember not to do anything that might jeopardize my role as mediator.

It is Natural to Blame the Mediator

It is natural for the parties to blame the mediator if the case does not get resolved. Who else are the parties going to blame? Generally parties are not going to go blame themselves, especially if they are thinking they are right and that there are "principles" involved. They are already mad at the other party so it makes sense that they would also get mad at the mediator if they things are not going the way they want. They transfer some of those bad feelings toward the mediator.

The Mediator Must Keep Track Of the Paperwork

Keeping track of the paperwork is even more important when communicating online. Emails are easily available so it is important to keep accurate track of offers and counter-offers. If the mediator does not keep track of where the mediation is, then the parties can easily bring up the pertinent emails to show what they said or agreed to at any point in time. It could be embarrassing if the parties show you are not on top of the paperwork.

G. The Mediator Must Know the Rhythm of an Online Mediation

The rhythm of an online mediation is very different from being in the same room. The mediator has to set the pace. The mediator cannot be too slow by not answering the emails in a timely manner. If one party takes days or even weeks to answer an email, it can make the pace so slow that the other side loses interest altogether. On the other hand, the mediator should not appear too eager and answer messages so quickly that it looks as though he is waiting at the computer for the party's next message. After a few emails, the mediator will develop an online rhythm.

H. Caucusing Online

Caucusing online is similar to caucusing in person. I have found that some parties are frustrated that they cannot see the other party's emails to me. Since there is a time lag, they want to be kept informed as to what is happening with the other side. Sometimes I will have to tell them that I have not gotten a message in the last couple of days and do not have anything to report. I have found the caucus is very useful in reporting the other side's offers. I am able to present the offer in a more favorable light than the way the party expressed it to me.

11

HOW TO MEDIATE IN THE WORKPLACE

here are many types of issues that can be mediated in the work place: sexual harass-
ent, co-worker conflicts, discrimination (gender, race, national origin, ethnicity,
ligion, or age,) work team conflicts, suspensions, terminations, promotions, and
lary increases. Usually mediation will take place by the boss, a human resources
ofessional, an eeo (equal employement opportunity) officer, an ombudsman (see
lossary) or an internal or external mediator. The first level of mediation is usually
e boss, who will mediate between two of his employees or mediate between one of
s supervisors and his employee. Either way, he will try to work things out, but if he
unsuccessful he may refer the situation to the human resources department.

Sometimes the human resources (HR) department will get a referral from a man-
er. HR professionals mediate disputes between employees every day although they
ight not call it mediation. They might call it counseling, conflict resolution, or
ndling a grievance. The HR professional usually meets with one employee first and
ks him what he wants to resolve the situation. Then at a later time, the HR profes-
nal will meet with the other party and see what they want. Sometimes the Human
sources professional will meet with both parties or continue to caucus with the two
les to see if a settlement can be fashioned. HR generally does not take sides but is
king for what is best for the company so the issue does not escalate to a higher
el.

The eeo officer investigates and resolves disputes based on gender, race, national
gin, religion, and age. He may do some mediation, but his role is much broader
n mediation since it includes investigation.

Some employers employ an ombudsperson who investigates complaints, mediates,
itrates, and facilitates disputes. The ombudsman concept originated in Sweden,
t it is now found world-wide. Often an ombudsman works on behalf of students
consumers who have complaints. The ombudsperson's powers are much broader
n the mediator's. While the mediator only mediates, the ombudsperson mediates,

investigates, and arbitrates. (For more information contact the International Ombudsman Association http://www.ombudsassociation.org/ or the United States Ombudsman Association http://www.usombudsman.org/)

An internal mediator is a mediator who works directly for the employer in a mediation program. The external mediator is called in for specific cases.

Here are some rules that apply in workplace mediations.

Don't Let The Parties Get Bogged Down By Emotion

It is especially important not to let the parties' emotions interfere with the mediation. One party may if angry because he was passed over for a promotion or did not get the raise he thought he deserved. It might be better to have the employee vent in caucus to allow these issues to be expressed so that the employee can move on. It is probably better do this in caucus so that the employee does not lose control in front of the boss. Otherwise, the boss will probably be glad he made the decision he did.

While in caucus, ask the employee to write down why he deserved the raise or promotion with concrete reasons with accomplishments and projects completed. The employee can also write down what they were told they needed to do to get the raise. While in caucus with the boss, ask the boss to say why he did not give the raise to the employee and what he told the employee what he needed to do to get the raise. Also ask the boss what he would need to do get a raise or promotion in the future. Then the mediator can help the parties get some common ground and see if something can be worked out without emotions interfering.

What do the parties want?

It is very important that the mediator find out what the parties want. Otherwise, the mediation can turn into a gripe session with no end or beginning. If the mediator asks the employee, what he wants, sometimes the answer will be, "I don't know." It is up to the mediator to make sure the employee knows what he wants to resolve the dispute. If somehow he has not given it much thought, the mediator will give him some questions and a short deadline to decide what is needed to end the situation. If the employee wants a raise or a promotion, he needs to give a reasoned explanation as to why he deserves it. If the employee feels that he has been unjustly treated, then the mediator can suggest a a resolution that would allow both parties to go forward. If the employee still does not know what he wants, then the mediation is going nowhere.

The Parties should do their research

If the mediation is about salary, the parties need to get financial information so they can find out what others in comparable positions are making within the company and in comparable positions in other companies. Each state's sunshine (open government) laws are different. For example Florida law is very liberal and public salaries are available to anyone who requests this information. The employee needs to compare himself to other employees in the same job classification with same credentials and same years of service. The employee can also look at that job title in other companies in the same locale or nationally if a high level position. The mediator should ask the parties to bring the employee handbook or other pertinent documents to the mediation.

Plan B

If one party is hoping to get a promotion, the mediator may suggest some alternatives. The employee needs to have a Plan B. What will the employee do if he does not get the promotion? Is he going to stay in the position anyway or start looking for a new job? Even if the employee wants to quit and look for a new job, assistance from his current employer or a good reference might be part of any settlement agreement. Maybe the employee will decide to go into a different field altogether. Sometimes the Plan B is a lot harder to determine than Plan A. When Plan A falls apart, it can be emotionally devastating. It is always good to have developed Plan B, C and D just in case the others do not work out. When you are dealing with your livelihood, it can be very disheartening to figure out alternatives.

Priorities

Although the promotion is of utmost importance to the employee, the boss may not have given it much thought. Mediating with the employee might be annoying, uncomfortable, boring, or even perceived as economically unadvisable. Instead of thinking about the employee's problems, the boss is probably thinking about his career and maybe even his issues at home. The boss may have financial constraints due to budget issues and may feel that his hands are tied regarding the employee's situation. The boss may be reluctant to change an employment action because of other employees waiting in the wings to have changes made for them. The boss may even agree that the employee deserves a raise, but the boss may feel he has to take the party line. The mediator may need to give a reality check to the employee so that he understands the real life context of the employment action.

Alternatives

If the boss is vehement that the employee will not get a promotion no matter what, the mediator may help suggest some alternatives. If the employee does not get the promotion, maybe he can at least get a raise. Can the employee get a provisional promotion and if it does not work out, go back to his current job? Can the employee do the duties of the new position but not get the raise for six months? Maybe the employee could ask for something else such as extra vacation days, flexible hours, telecommuting, extended leave of absence, or travel to a national conference. If none of these alternatives stick, then the employee may have to go to Plan B.

Step back and look at the big picture

When something happens at work like not getting a raise or partnership, the mediator can help the parties reflect on the big picture. Can I stay here and work out these issues with my boss? Or is this a good time to throw in the towel and go with another company or with another type of employer? Where do I want to be five years from now or fifteen years from now? Do I want to be self-employed where I make my own decisions? Was this really a blessing in disguise? Am I better off knowing that this job is not for me so I can go in another direction with my life? Your answers to these questions will help you decide the direction of your next move. Sometimes leaving is the best option.

12

IF MEDIATION FAILS, SHOULD YOU GO TO ARBITRATION?

certain number of mediations will reach impasse and the deadlock cannot be bro-
n by the parties despite their best efforts. If this is a court-ordered mediation, the
se will go forward and be heard by the judge. If this is not a court-ordered media-
n, then the parties will need to make a decision as to whether they want to go to
other forum such as arbitration.

ould you go to Arbitration?

bitration is a process where parties present their arguments in a hearing format to
arbitrator who makes the decision. By going to arbitration, they have given the
cision-making power to the arbitrator, who acts as a judge. The arbitration hearing
much more informal than court. Arbitration can either be binding or nonbinding.
bor/management arbitration is binding, which means that the decision cannot be
pealed or overturned unless the arbitrator showed bias, discrimination, or fraud in
decision. The courts have long recognized that labor arbitrators have a specialized
owledge of labor law that judges generally do not have. An arbitration that is not
ling means that the parties can reject the decision. The parties have the option of
ing to court or even to another arbitrator. The non-binding decision is an indepen-
t assessment of the case and may be used in settlement later on. The parties may
t take a non-binding arbitration seriously if they have the power to reject the deci-
n. The parties need to look at how much they are willing to spend and how impor-
t the final resolution is to them before deciding how to proceed.

hat Are The Differences Between Mediation And Arbitration?

diation: The parties agree to work with a facilitator or mediator to resolve a dis-
e.

itration: Parties agree to present their arguments to an arbitrator for a ruling.

Mediation: The parties control the outcome.
Arbitration: The parties do not control the outcome.

Mediation: The mediator does not make a decision.
Arbitration: The arbitrator makes a decision.

Mediation: The mediator asks questions to help the parties settle the case.
Arbitration: The arbitrator asks questions in order to make a ruling.

Mediation: The decision-making power is retained by the parties.
Arbitration: The arbitrator weighs the evidence and makes a decision.

Mediation: The mediator has no vested interest in the proceeding.
Arbitration: The arbitrator has no vested interest in the proceeding.

What are the advantages of binding arbitration over going directly to court?

1. The arbitrator usually has special expertise that a judge does not.

2. Arbitration usually takes less time than going through the court system.

3. The costs of arbitration are usually much less than going to court.

4. The proceedings are more private than court if the parties don't want publicity.

5. There is more flexibility in scheduling the arbitration than scheduling in court.

6. A binding arbitration decision is generally easier to enforce than a court order.

7. A binding decision can only be appealed under very limited circumstances such as arbitrator bias or fraud

What are the disadvantages of going to binding arbitration?

1. An arbitration can be costly especially if there is an arbitration panel.

2. An arbitration may take as long as a court case if there are scheduling difficulties

3. The parties may disagree with the decision, but unless the arbitrator exhibits bias or fraud, the parties are stuck with it.

The arbitrator does not have to go by precedent. The arbitrator makes the decision based on this case only.

Alternate Dispute Resolution (known as ADR), is an alternative to taking a case to urt. Collectively, procedures such as negotiation, mediation, arbitration, med/arbition and arb/mediation are a cheaper and faster alternative to litigation. In addi-n, the parties have more control of the outcome of the case, especially in gotiation or mediation. ADR is preferable to going to court when the parties must rk with each other after the hearing, such as the parents in child custody or visita-n cases. The conflict and animosity between the parents could be increased as a ult of an adversarial process.

hat is Mediation/Arbitration?

ediation/arbitration, known as med-arb, is a hybrid process. An arbitrator is cho-, and if both parties agree, he will mediate the case first and then if that does not olve the case, he will arbitrate the case and make a decision. The advantage is that same person can mediate and arbitrate. The disadvantage is that the arbitrator y learn things about the case in the mediation phase that might affect the arbitra-n decision. If that is an initial concern, then the parties can go to traditional medi-on and then if the case is not resolved through mediation, they can go to an an itrator who knows nothing about the case.

hat is Arbitration/Mediation?

oitration/mediation, known as arb/med, is a hybrid process that is the reverse of diation/arbitration. The arbitration takes place first and the arbitrator writes a ision but does not show it to the parties. Then the same person acts as the media- and conducts the mediation. If the mediation resolves the dispute, then the writ- decision is not revealed. If the mediation is not resolved, then the arbitrator's tten opinion is shown to the parties who are bound by the decision. The advan- e of doing the arbitration first is that the arbitrator's decision is not influenced by ormation he may receive later in a mediation. This is why some prefer arb/med r med/arb. On the other hand, some might say it is a waste of time and money if mediation phase resolves the case and the arbitration decision is not used. How- r, the parties may be more motivated in resolving the mediation themselves rather n waiting to see what the arbitrator's decision is.

hat is The Difference Between Mediation/Arbitration (Med/Arb) and bitration/Mediation (Arb/Med)?

diation-Arbitration, known as Med/Arb, is a hybrid process.

Arbitration/Mediation, known as Arb/Med, is a hybrid process.

Med/Arb: An arbitrator is chosen who mediates the case first. The advantage of doing the mediation first is that if resolved, there is no arbitration.
Arb/Med: The arbitration takes place first. The advantage of doing the arbitration first is that the arbitrator is not influenced by information he may receive later in confidential caucus in mediation.

Med/Arb: If the mediation is successful, there is no arbitration.
Arb/Med: The arbitration takes place regardless, but the arbitration decision is not revealed if the mediation is successful.

Med/Arb: An advantage is that the two processes can be done by the same person.
Arb/Med: An advantage is that the two processes can be done by the same person.

Med/Arb: A disadvantage is that the mediator may learn things in the mediation that might affect his decision in the arbitration.
Arb/Med: The disadvantage is time, expense, and energy for the arbitrator's opinion when it is not revealed because the mediation is successful.

What are the Advantages of Med/Arb or Arb/Med Over Mediating and Arbitrating Separately?

1. The parties know that the case will be resolved, one way or the other.

2. Generally the costs are lower when the same neutral is mediator and arbitrator

3. Generally it takes less time when the same person is mediator and arbitrator

What is an Ombudsperson?

An ombudsperson is usually a government or corporate official appointed to investigate complaints, mediate, arbitrate and facilitate disputes. The ombudsman concept originated in Sweden, but it is now found world-wide. Often an ombudsman works on behalf of students or consumers who have complaints. The ombudsperson's powers are much broader than the Mediator's. While the Mediator only mediates, the Ombudsperson mediates, investigates and arbitrates. (For more information contact the International Ombudsman Association http://www.ombudsassociation.org/ or the United States Ombudsman Association http://www.usombudsman.org/)

What Are The Differences Between Mediator and Ombudsman?

An Ombudsman investigates complaints and mediates, arbitrates and facilitates disputes. Mediation is only one of ombudsman's roles.

Mediation: The mediator has only one role: mediator.
Ombudsman: An ombudsman has many roles. In addition to mediation, he also, investigates, arbitrates, facilitates and makes recommendations.

Mediation: The mediator makes no reports.
Ombudsman: The ombudsman makes reports.

Mediation: After the mediation is over, the mediator does not follow up.
Ombudsman: The ombudsman can remain in contact with the parties.

Mediator: The mediator is independent, impartial, and confidential.
Ombudsman: The ombudsman is independent, impartial, and confidential.

Mediator: The mediator can help the parties identify options.
Ombudsman: The ombudsman can help the parties identify options.

Appendix A

Mediator's Opening Statement

Preliminaries

. Introduction of Mediator: My name is Mary Greenwood and I am your Mediator
·day.

. Introduction of parties
What are the first and last names of the parties?
How are the names pronounced?
What are the mailing addresses and telephone numbers of the
.rties?
How do parties want to be addressed? first name or last name? Mrs.? Ms? Doctor?
Is anyone missing?
Is anyone observing?
Who are witnesses?
Are there attorneys present?

What is Mediation?
ediation is a way to resolve problems by mutual agreeing to use a third-party neu-
l or facilitator. The mediator helps the parties identify the issues, search for solu-
ns, and facilitate voluntary agreements between the parties. The parties make the
:isions not the mediator.

Mediation terms: (See Appendix B)
I will try to explain all mediation terms when I first use them.
If a term is unfamiliar to you, please let me know.
Some of these terms may mean something different from their regular usage in
glish.

II. Mediator's Responsibilities

E. What are the Mediator's Roles?

1. As the mediator, my role is facilitator.
2. My job is to help the parties resolve the dispute.
3. I do not make a ruling like a judge or arbitrator.
4. I do not give legal advice.
5. I am not a therapist.

F. Neutrality of mediator

1. I do not represent either party.
2. I don't take sides.
3. I don't make a suggestion for a solution unless requested by both parties.
4. If I spend more time in a caucus with one party, that does not mean I am favoring that party. I may just have more questions.

G. Confidentiality

1. When I meet with you individually in caucus, I will ask you questions about the issues and your answers will be kept confidential.
2. I will not tell the other side anything that you do not want me to tell them. (For example, you may tell me that you want $100 but will take $80. I would tell the other side that you want $100 and would not say that you would be satisfied with $80 unless you specifically authorized me to divulge that.)
3. I make the commitment to both of you that I will not divulge any information to the other party unless you have authorized it.
4. After the mediation is over, I will not discuss any details of the mediation and ask that you do the same.
5. Communications made during the mediation process are confidential unless required or permitted by law (Florida mediation requirement.)

H. Ethics

1. I pledge to conduct this mediation in an ethical manner.
2. I will be fair, objective, and unbiased.
3. I will discuss the case only in mediation sessions.
4. I will only discuss the case with both parties present or during a scheduled caucus with one party.
5. If you see something that you perceive as unethical, please bring it to my attention so we can discuss further.

II. Parties' Rights and Responsibilities

, Self-Determination

. Decisions made during mediation are to be made by the parties not the mediator.

. The mediator is not allowed to coerce or unduly influence the parties in making their decisions.

, As the mediator, I can make suggestions or propose alternatives, but the ultimate decision is up to you.

, If I determine that one party cannot make those kinds of decisions, then it is my responsibility to close or postpone the case.

Voluntariness

, Mediation is voluntary.

, Either side can decide to discontinue the mediation.

. Authority

, It is very important that both parties have binding authority to resolve the case

, I am going to ask you some questions to see if you do have authority.

V. Mediation Mechanics

, Caucusing

From time to time I will meet with each of you separately so that you can speak freely to me without the other party being present.

This allows you to tell me what your position and fallback positions are.

This will allow me to talk to you candidly without the other side being present.

. Questions

I will be asking you questions to help me understand the situation.

If you want to know why I am asking a certain question, please ask me.

If you have any questions about the proceedings, please ask me.

There is no such thing as a stupid question.

, Impasse:

We reach an impasse when we are deadlocked and no agreement can be reached.

I can suggest a possible solution or

I can close the case which puts us at the same place we were at the start of the mediation.

V. Procedural Issues

O. Groundrules:
1. We will use common rules of courtesy. Only one person will speak at a time.
2. No one will use profanity.
3. Meetings will start on time.
4. Cell-phones will be turned off during mediation and can only be used during breaks
5. Either party can request a caucus, but the mediator will make the final decision.
6. Both parties agree to comply with reasonable requests for information.
7. The party requesting the information agrees to pay reproduction costs.
8. The parties agree to discuss and confirm the date of their next mediation session at the close of every session.

P. Note-taking
1. I will be taking notes throughout the mediation.
2. This does not mean I am not listening.
3. These notes help me keep track of where we are in the mediation.
4. This is helpful for me when we start each subsequent session.
5. These are my notes which I do not share with anyone and they are only taken to help me facilitate the case.

Q. Housekeeping issues
1. Where are the bathrooms?
2. When is lunch?
3. Cell phone policy
4. When will we finish?
5. When will we take breaks?
6. When will we caucus?
7. Where do you go when other side is caucusing
8. How long will each session be?

R. Opening statements by parties in joint session
1. Both parties will make an opening statement.
2. Please include what you want in your opening statement.
3. I will ask for volunteers to go first. If no one volunteers or both volunteer, I will do a coin toss.

S. Rules for attorneys, if present
Since one or both of you are represented by attorneys, I have the following rule:

The parties will speak for themselves, not the attorneys
If you wish to speak with your attorney before answering, request a caucus with
ur attorney.

Appendix B

Glossary Terms

Alternate Dispute Resolution, known as ADR, includes negotiation, mediation, and arbitration and other dispute procedures that are an alternative to going to court. Generally ADR is faster and less expensive than litigation. Generally the parties have more control of the outcome than if they filed a court case.

Arbitration is a process where parties present their arguments to a neutral arbitrator who makes the decision. This is an alternative to litigation (going to court) and is one of the procedures known as alternate dispute resolution, or ADR. Labor/management arbitration is one of the oldest kinds of arbitration. The arbitrator is like a judge, while the parties make their own decisions in mediation and negotiation.

Arbitration/Mediation (Arb/Med) is a hybrid process where the arbitration takes place first and both parties present their case. The arbitrator writes an arbitration decision but does not show it to the parties. Then the arbitrator becomes the mediator and conducts the mediation. If the mediation is resolved, then the written decision is not revealed. If the mediation is not resolved, then the arbitrator's written decision will be revealed. The advantage of doing the arbitration first is that the arbitrator is not influenced by information he may receive later in the mediation.

Authority means that the person negotiating has the legal power to make a decision and act on behalf of his employer. Even if a person has authority, it might only be authority up to a certain amount. It is better to know what the person's authority is before the negotiations start. If someone does not have authority, then there is no point negotiating with him because he cannot approve any agreement.

Bargaining Chips are concessions that can be offered to the other side as an incentive to get something. Using the poker terminology makes the term a metaphor for the negotiation process. One should always keep some bargaining chips in reserve because they may be needed to close the deal.

Binding Arbitration is a type of arbitration where the arbitrator's decision is final and cannot be appealed by the parties unless the arbitrator committed fraud or showed bias.

Boulewareism is a take it or leave it approach to negotiation. The term is named after Lemuel Boulware, a vice-president at General Electric in the 1950's. After much research as to what was best for the company, he opened the negotiations with his first, last and best offer and told the electrical union to take it or leave it. The court later determined that this one-sided approach was not good faith bargaining because there was no give and take by the parties and no involvement by the union. (This is sometimes spelled **Boulewarism.**)

Caucuses are meetings held by a mediator separately with each party to discuss the mediation. It allows the party to talk about the dispute without the other party being present.

Concessions are giving something up that the other party wants. The term is used synonymously with bargaining chips. You made too many concessions and don't have any bargaining chips left.

Confidentiality means that information concerning the negotiation is not divulged or discussed with outside parties during the negotiations. Breaking confidentiality can jeopardize the negotiation process. It is important to make confidentiality part of the groundrules for the negotiation. It is also important that all team members understand their obligation to keep proceedings confidential.

Decoys are used to mislead and lure an unsuspecting bird by setting out a realistic duck model so the bird will follow the decoy and allow hunters to shoot at him. The same tactic is used in negotiations. The purpose is to mislead the unsuspecting party with a diversionary tactic which is the decoy. This is similar to the smoke screen and red herring.

Deadlock occurs when the parties reach an *impasse* and there does not appear to be any room for agreement. The impasse has to be broken or the mediation will be closed without resolution.

Devil's Advocate approach is a way to give a reality check to the other side and point out the flaws in his arguments. The expression is *Let me play the devil's advocate.* I

aying, one is insulated from criticism because the mediator is pointing out these
oblems as if he were the devil or a third party.

iscrimination is treating a person adversely because of their race, religion, color,
ability, gender, age or national origin.

iversity acknowledges differences in culture and experiences. This can include age,
nnicity, class, gender, race, sexual orientation, religion, geographical location,
come, marital status, and work experience.

ce-saving is a way to allow someone to get out of an embarrassing situation with
dignity intact. Giving someone a way out is a tradition in many Asian countries.
u are helping the other side look good and not be humiliated.

edback is a system that allows eBay users to rate the buyer or seller in each eBay
nsaction. A buyer or seller can leave a positive, neutral, or negative rating with a
mment to explain their satisfaction level. The feedback score is the sum of all of the
ings an eBay user received from individual users. The positive number is compared
the negative to give the user a percentage number as well. For example, a perfect
re of all positives is 100%.

nal offer is the last offer made in a negotiation. Don't call it a final offer if you
ve anything else to negotiate. Do not use the final offer at the beginning of negoti-
ons. This is also called Boulwareism or the take or leave it approach. There should
ly be one final offer and it should be used to close the deal at the end of negotia-
ns.

od faith bargaining is required by federal and state labor laws. It means that the
ties have a duty to approach bargaining with the right attitude and are prepared to
cuss issues and meet on a regular basis. It does not mean that the parties have to
ne to an agreement though. Good faith bargaining is the opposite of Boulwareism
d take it or leave it.

oundrules are the procedural rules that are used for the negotiation process and
eed to by both parties. Here are some examples: Only one person will speak at a
e. Parties will be courteous at all times. Having groundrules helps the negotiation
more smoothly because all parties know the expectations in advance. This can be
luded in your opening statement.

Impasse occurs when the parties are deadlocked and there does not appear to be any room for agreement. The impasse has to be broken or the mediation will have to be closed without resolution.

Lagniappe is Creole term used in Louisiana, meaning an unexpected gift, benefit, or dollop which is given by a shopkeeper to add a little bonus to the purchase. In mediation each party wants to get something extra. The word is derived from Spanish "la napa" which means gift and from Quecha, a native South American language "yapay" which means to give more. The term got a French spelling via New Orleans.

Mediation is a process where parties use a neutral facilitator called a mediator to help the parties resolve their dispute. The parties do not deal with each other directly as in a negotiation. The mediator does not make a decision as an arbitrator or judge does. The parties resolve the case with the mediator's assistance. Mediation is a type of alternate dispute resolution, which is an alternative to going to court.

Mediation/Arbitration (Med/Arb) is a hybrid process. An arbitrator is chosen and if both parties agree, he will mediate the case first. If that does not work, he will arbitrate the case and make a decision. The advantage of med/arb is that both processes are done by the same person. The disadvantage is that the arbitrator may learn things about the case in the mediation phase that might affect the arbitration decision.

Negotiation is a process where parties resolve disputes with each other. The term is often used synonymously with bargaining. The essence of the negotiation is that both parties agree to work with each other to resolve a problem or dispute. Negotiation is a type of alternate dispute resolution, which is an alternative to going to court.

Negotiating against yourself occurs when someone makes another offer when there already is an offer on the table. If the person negotiating does not wait for a counter offer, he will be negotiating against himself. For example, you offer $5000 and then you offer $10,000 after you do not get a response. If you had asked for a counter offer instead, the other party might have countered with $7500 and you would have gained $2500. Never make two offers in a row. Always ask for a counter-offer.

Neutrality means that the mediator has no involvement or personal interest in the case. The mediator is fair, honest, ethical, and shows no bias. In addition the mediator starts the case with an open mind.

Non-binding Arbitration is a type of arbitration where the arbitration decision is not binding on the parties. The parties can still go to court or even request another arbitration. It is, in effect, an independent assessment of the case which might help in resolving the dispute.

An **Ombudsman** is a person who investigates complaints and also mediates, arbitrates, and facilitates disputes. Mediation is only one of the ombudsman's roles. (For more information contact the United States Ombudsman Association at http://www.usombudsman.org/ or the International Ombudsman Association at http://www.ombudsassociation.org/)

Online Dispute Resolution, known as ODR, is a way to resolve disputes online and the online equivalent of alternate dispute resolution. Online mediation is the most common form of ODR, but there is online negotiation and arbitration as well. Online mediation is not done in real time like face to face mediation. ODR uses technology and its usage will increase and probably be as common as regular ADR.

Package Offer is a way to put several proposals on the table to make the deal look more attractive. I will give you A and B and C but we want D and E. This is sometimes called Bundling and is more complex than a simple trade-off.

Phishing is a fake website. Internet users are lured through lookalike emails from AOL, PayPal, eBay, and banks asking for confidential account information. That information is used to access someone's account and steal his identity.

Quid pro quo means this for that in Latin. In negotiations, it means I will give you what you want if you give me what I want. It is basically the same as a tradeoff. Both parties can get what they want and the problem is solved.

Red herring is a tactic to mislead the other party and create a diversion. The origin of the term involved rubbing a red herring on hounds to protect the hunted fox. The hounds will smell the herring and won't be able to track the fox. A red herring is essentially a false clue or pony issue used to distract hounds, politicians, and negotiators. This is similar to a decoy and smoke screen.

Saving face is a way to allow someone their dignity and not be humiliated. Allowing someone to retire rather than firing them is a way to save face.

Self-Determination means that decisions made during the mediation are to be made by the parties not the mediator. The mediator's job is to help facilitate the mediation but the mediator cannot exert coercion or undue influence on the parties to resolve the case a certain way.

Smoke screen is a way to mask one's true intent and create a diversion. In war, smoke is released to mask the location or moving of troops. In negotiations, it is a diversionary tactic to take attention away from the main objective and give attention to something of little or no importance. This is similar to the decoy and red herring.

Spoof is an internet-based scheme to steal someone's identity. An email, that looks like an official email from eBay, a bank, Paypal, or Aol, lures the person to a fake website (phishing) with the purpose of tricking that person into giving confidential account information.

Take it or leave it is an approach used to give the other side a first, last, and firm offer. Basically this approach means that the party is not going to negotiate. This is risky approach especially at the beginning of negotiations. It should only be used at the end of negotiations to close the deal (See final offer and Boulwareism.)

Tentative Agreement, (TA) is used as a way to tentatively agree on each proposal. It is understood that changes could still be made in the final version, but it is a good faith method to keep track of what has been agreed to.

Tradeoff is the same as quid pro quo. In mediation, it means I will give you what you want if you give me what I want. Both parties can get what they want and the problem is solved.

Venting is a way to express emotions like anger and frustration so that the parties are ready for mediation. It is a way to let go of emotions and clear the way for mediation to take place. Often the first session of mediation will let the parties vent so that the process can go to the next step.

Voluntarism means that both parties in the mediation voluntarily agree to try to resolve the dispute. Either party can decide to stop the mediation at any time.

Walkaway is a variation of the take it or leave it approach. If you don't give me what want, then I will quit or walk away.

Unfair Labor Practice is a violation of federal or state labor law.

APPENDIX C

WHAT MAKES A GOOD MEDIATOR?

Neutral

Calm, Cool, Collected

Creative

Ethical

Fair

Firm

Flexible

Good Listener

Honest

Knowledgeable

Patient

Perceptive

Persistent

Personable

Reasonable

Respectful

17. Sense of Humor

18. Sincere

19. Thinks Before Speaking

APPENDIX D
DO'S AND DON'TS OF MEDIATORS

O'S

Be Appreciative of time and effort

Be Calm

Be Confident

Be Confidential

Be in Control

Be Courteous

Be Flexible

Be a Good Listener

Delay if Necessary

Be Honest

Be Positive

Be Prepared

Be Tactful

Have a Poker Face

Keep Session on Track

16. Read between the lines

17. Give a Reality Check

DON'T

1. Argue with the parties

2. Give your opinion unless requested

3. Say who is right or wrong

4. Make a decision for the parties

5. Assume

6. Badmouth the other side

7. Assess Blame

8. Be Patronizing

9. Compromise your principles

10. Interrupt

11. Let Down Your Guard

12. Lie

13. Lose Your Temper

14. Make Promises you cannot keep

15. Rush either side

16. Coerce

17. Underestimate the other side

APPENDIX E

INTERNATIONAL, NATIONAL, AND STATE MEDIATION RESOURCES

ational and International Resources
nerican Arbitration Association: www.adr.org
nerican College of Civil Trial Mediators: www.acctm.org
ampus ADR Organization: http://www.campus-adr.org/
ternational Association of Mediators and Arbitrators: http://www.e-iama.com/
ediation Canada: www.mediationcanada.org
ational Association for Community Mediation: http://www.nafcm.org/pg35.cfm
ie Ombudsman Association: http://web.mit.edu/negotiation/toa/TOAintro.html
solute Systems: http://www.resolutesystems.com/About/
arch for Common Ground: http://www.sfcg.org/
K-European Mediation Association: www.mediarcom.com
sociation for Conflict Resolution: http://www.acrnet.org/
nerican Bar Association, Conflict Resolution Section: www.abanet.org/dispute
ternational Academy of Mediators (Toronto): www.iamed.org
ediators Without Borders: http://www.mediatorswithoutborders.org/

ite Resources

ibama
ibama Center For Dispute Resolution
) Box 671
ontgomery, AL 36101
one: (334) 269-0409
p://alabamaadr.org/

Alaska

Dispute Resolution Coordinator
Alaska Court System
820 W. 4th Street, Room 223
Anchorage, AK 99501
(907) 264-8236
(907) 264-8291 fax

Alaska Dispute Settlement Association
P.O. Box 242922
Anchorage, AK 99524-2922 USA
Phone: (907) 258-0624
Email: jbressers@alaska.com
Website: www.adsa.ws/home.htm

Arizona
ADR Director
Superior Court of Arizona
201 W. Jefferson, CCB5
Phoenix, AZ 85003
(602) 506-0199

Arkansas
Arkansas ADR Commission
625 Marshall St.
Little Rock, AR 72201
Phone: 501-682-9400
http://courts.state.ar.us/courts/adr.html

California
Northern California Mediation Association: http://www.mediate.com/
Southern California Mediation Association
10850 Wilshire Blvd
Suite 400
Los Angeles, CA 90024 USA
Phone: 1-877-9MEDIATE Fax: 714-669-9341
Email: scma@scmediation.org
Website: www.scmediation.org

Colorado
Colorado Council of Mediators (CCMO)
5399 So Fiddlers Green Circle
Suite 102
Greenwood Village, CO 80111-4974 USA
Phone: 303-322-9275
Email: ccmo@coloradomediation.org
Website: http://www.coloradomediation.org

Connecticut
ADR Programs,
Caseflow Management Specialist at (860) 263-2734, ext. 3035 or
Catherine.Lapollo@jud.ct.gov

Connecticut State Board of Mediation and Arbitration: http://www.ctdol.state.ct.us/
medarb/default.htm

Delaware
Delaware State Bar Association ADR Section http://www.dsba.
org/SecComm/AltDisRes/Altdisres.htm

Florida
Florida Academy of Professional Mediators
Website: http://www.tfapm.org/

Association of South Florida Mediators and Arbitrators
Website: http://asfma.org/index.htm

Dispute Resolution Center,
Supreme Court Building,
Tallahassee, Florida 32399,
850-921-2910, fax 850-922-9290
Website: http://www.flcourts.org/gen_public/adr/index.shtml

Georgia
Georgia Commission on Dispute Resolution Website:
http://www.state.ga.us/gadr/adr_orgs.html

Georgia Bar Association Dispute Resolution Section Website:
http://www.gabar.org/sections/section_web_pages/

Hawaii
Center for Alternative Dispute Resolution
State of Hawaii Judiciary
417 S. King St., Room 207
Honolulu, HI 96813

Idaho
Idaho Mediation Association
PO Box 2504,
Boise, Id 83701
Tel. 208-0855-0506
Email: info@idahomediation.org
Website: www.idahomediation.org

Illinois
Center for Conflict Resolution
11 East Adams Suite 500 Chicago, Illinois 60603
Phone: 312.922.6464 Fax: 312.922.6463
E-mail: ccr@ccrchicago.org

Mediation Council of Illinois (Family)
PO Box 97
Cary, Il 60013
Tel. 312-641-3000
Website: www.mediationcouncilofillinois.org

Indiana
Indiana State Bar, Dispute Resolution Section
http://www.inbar.org/default.asp

Iowa
Iowa State Bar ADR Section:
Chair,
317 Sixth Ave, Suite 1200
Des Moines, IA 50309-4195
Phone: (515) 288-6041

ax: (515) 246-1474 fanter@whitfieldlaw.com
ttp://www.iowabar.org/main.nsf

Kansas
Dispute Resolution Coordinator
Office of Judicial Administration
01 W. 10th
Topeka, KS 66612-1507
thompsona@kscourts.org
85-291-3748

Kentucky
DR Director
Administrative Office of the Courts
00 Millcreek Park
Frankfort, KY 40601
02) 573-0327
02) 573-169 Fax
PretrialServices@mail.aoc.ky.us

Mediation Association of Kentucky
101 Bardstown Rd.
Louisville, KY 40205 USA
Phone: x
Email: info@kymediation.org
Website: www.kymediation.org

Louisiana
Louisana State Bar
Website: http://www.lsba.org/

Maine
Director, Court ADR Service of the State of Maine
Judicial Branch
7 New Meadows Road
West Bath, ME 04530-9704
07) 442-0227
07) 442-0228 Fax

Maine Assn of Dispute Resolution Professionals
PO Box 8187
Portland, ME 04104 USA
Phone: 1-877-265-9712
Email: nmark@usm.maine.edu
Website: www.madrp.org

Maine Association of Mediators
execdir@mainemediators.org www.mainemediators.org/

Maryland
Director, Maryland Alternative Dispute Commission, 120 East Chesapeake Avenue,2nd Floor, chambers 6, Towson MD 21286, 410-3212398, 410 321-2399 (fax)

Massachusetts
Administrative Attorney/ADR Coordinator
Administrative Office of the Trial Courts
Two Center Plaza Room 540
Boston, MA 02108
(617) 742-8575
(617) 742-0968 fax

Director, Massachusetts Office of Dispute Resolution (MODR)
One Ashburnton Place, Room 501
Boston, MA 02108
Jeghelian.susan@state.ma.us

Michigan
Office of Dispute Resolution
Michigan State Court Administrative Office
309 N. Washington Square
P.O. Box 30048
Lansing, MI 48909
(517) 373-4839
(517) 373-8922 fax

Dispute Resolution Association of Michigan
Lansing, MI 48912 USA
Phone: 517.248.2274

mail: resolve@tds.net
Website: www.michiganresolution.org

Minnesota
Director, ADR Program
Supreme Court of Minnesota
20 Minnesota Judicial Center
5 Rev. Dr. Martin Luther King Jr. Boulevard
. Paul, MN 55155
51) 297-7590
51) 297-1173 Fax

Mississippi
OC Director
Administrative Office of the Courts
O. Box 117
ckson, MS 39205
01) 354-7449
01) 354-7459 Fax

Missouri
mily Preservation Project Specialist
ffice of the State Courts Administrator
12 Industrial Drive
O. Box 104480
ferson City, MO 65110
73) 751-4377
73) 522-6086 Fax
ahm@osca.state.mo.us
sociation of Missouri Mediators
O. Box 22373
nsas City, MO 64113 USA
one: 816-736-8402
nail: momediators@mediate.com
ebsite: www.mediate.com/amm
tegories: Membership Organizations, Newsletter
Non-profit Organization

Montana

Clerk of the Supreme Court
Justice Building
P.O. Box 203003
Helena, MT 59620-3003
(406) 444-3858
(406) 444-5705 Fax
Montana Mediation Association
P.O. Box 6363
Great Falls, MT 59406 USA
Phone: 406-727-8365
Email: memberservices@mtmediation.org
Website: www.mtmediation.org

Nebraska
Nebraska Mediation Center Association: **http://www.nemediation.org/**

Nebraska State Bar Association, Alternate Dispute Resolution Section: **http:/ www.nebar.com/**

Nevada
Manager, Southern Region
Family Mediation and Assessment Center
Family Court and Services Center
601 North Pecos Road
Las Vegas, NV 89101
(702) 455-4186
gamble@co.clark.nv.us

Director of Court Mediation
Northern Region
Family Mediation Program
Courthouse
75 Court Street
Reno, NV 89501
(775) 328-3556

New Hampshire
Clerk of Court
Chair of Superior Court ADR Committee

2 Main Street
ewport, NH 03773
03) 863-3450
03) 863-3204 Fax
volfe@Courts.State.NH.US

ew Jersey
anager, Special Programs Unit
dministrative Office of the Courts
ughes Justice Complex
O. Box 988
enton, NJ 08625
09) 984-2172
09) 633-7142 Fax
arilyn.slivka@judiciary.state.nj.us

ordinator
DR Program Operations
dministrative Office of the Courts
ughes Justice Complex
O. Box 988
enton, NJ 08625
09) 984-2337
09) 633-7142 Fax
w Jersey Association of Professional Mediators
3 Towne Centre Drive
llsborough, NJ 08844 USA
one: 800-981-4800
ail: info@njapm.org
bsite: www.njapm.org

w Mexico
rk, Second District Court
unty Courthouse
D. Box 488
uquerque, NM 87103
5) 841-7425
5) 841-7446 Fax
lbas@jidmail.nmcourts.com

New Mexico Mediation Association:
P.O. Box 82384
Albuquerque, NM 87198
(505) 466-1804
http://www.nmma.info/
nmmasecretary@nmma.info

New York
State ADR Coordinator
New York State Unified Court System
25 Beaver Street, Room 855
New York, NY 10004
(212) 428-2863
(212) 428-2696 Fax
dweitz@courts.state.ny.us

The New York State Dispute Resolution Association
255 River Street
4th Floor
Troy, NY 12180 USA
Phone: 518/687-2240
Email: nysdra@nysdra.org
Website: www.nysdra.org

North Carolina
Executive Secretary
State of North Carolina Dispute Resolution Commission
P.O. Box 2448
Raleigh, NC 27602 Mailing Address
(919) 981-5077
(919) 981-5048 Fax
l eslier@aoc.state.nc.us

Mediation Network of North Carolina:
Post Office Box 648
Siler City, NC 27344
Phone 919-663-5650
Email: mnnc@mnnc.org

North Dakota
Executive Director
State Bar Association of North Dakota
P.O. Box 2136
Bismarck, ND 58502
(701) 255-1404
(701) 224-1621 Fax
http://www.court.state.nd.us/court/adr/
Website for Supreme Court of North Dakota includes link to a statewide ADR neutral roster.

Ohio
Supreme Court of Ohio
5 South Front Street, Sixth Floor,
Columbus, Oh 43215-3431
Tel. 614-387-9420
Email: mediate@sconet.state.oh.us
http://www.sconet.state.oh.us/dispute_resolution/

Ohio Mediation Association **http://www.mediate.com/ohio/**
897 Liberty Bell Lane
Reynoldsburg, OH 43068 USA
Phone: 614/863-4775 Fax: 614/863-4775
Email: cradigan@insight.rr.com
Website: www.mediate.com/ohio

Oklahoma
Director
Alternative Dispute Resolution System of Oklahoma
Administrative Office of the Courts
1915 North Stiles, Suite 305
Oklahoma City, OK 73105
(405) 521-2450
(405) 521-6815 fax
e.tate@oscn.net

Oregon
Mediation Coordinator

Oregon Judicial Department
1163 State Street
Salem, OR 97301-2563
(503) 986.4539
(503) 986.6419 fax
Oregon Mediatin AssociationPO Box 2592
Portland, OR 97208 USA
Phone: 503-872-9775 Fax: 503-245-5998
Email: omediate@teleport.com
Website: www.omediate.org

Pennsylvania
Pennsylvania Council of Mediators: www.pamediation.org/

Rhode Island
Volunteer Center for Rhode Island
http://www.volunteersolutions.org/vcri/org/221827.html

South Carolina
State Bar Association, Dispute Resolution Center, no website

South DakotaSouth Dakota Mediation Association
Dakota Hall 119—USD
414 E. Clark Street
Vermillion, SD 57069-2390 USA
Phone: x
Email: dspader@usd.edu
Website: www.usd.edu/sdma/main.htm

Tennessee
Tennesse Association of Professional Mediators:
PO Box 150626
Nashville, TN 37215-0626
Phone: 615-292-6069
http://www.tennmediators.org/

Texas
Texas Association of Mediators
P. O. Box 191208

Dallas, TX 75219-8208 USA
Phone: x
Email: jillmckibben@earthlink.net
Website: www.txmediator.org

Utah
Director of ADR
Administrative Office of the Courts
P.O. Box 140241
Salt Lake City, UT 84114-0241
(801) 578-3984
(801) 578-3843 fax
cathye@email.utcourts.gov

Vermont
Vermont Bar Association http://www.vtbar.org/index.asp
District of Vermont Early Neutral Evaluation: http://www.fjc.gov/public/home.nsf/
autoframe?openform&url_l=/public/home.
nsf/inavgeneral?openpage&url_r=/public/home.nsf/pages/785

Virginia
Director of Dispute Resolution Services
Supreme Court of Virginia,
Department of Dispute Resolution Services
Office of the Executive Secretary
100 N. Ninth Street, Third Floor,
Richmond, VA 32319
804-786-6455 gravindra@courts.state.va.us

Washington
Washington State Bar ADR: http://www.wsba.org/lawyers/services/adr.htm
Washington Mediation Association
422 Pike Street, PMB #1095
Seattle, WA 98122-3934 USA
Phone: (509) 324-9052
Email: washingtonmediation@earthlink.net
Website: www.washingtonmediation.org

West Virginia

West Virginia Human Rights Commission Mediation: http://www.wvf.state.wv.us/
wvhrc/mediation%20process.htm
West Virginia Bar Trained Mediators: http://www.wvbar.
org/barinfo/services/mediators.htm

Wisconsin
Wisconsin Association of Mediators
P.O. Box 44578
Madison, WI 53744-4578 USA
Phone: (608) 277-1771
Email: wam@mailbag.com
Website: www.wamediators.org

Wisconsin Court System Mediation and ADR: http://www.wicourts.gov/services/
attorney/mediation.htm

Wyoming
Chief U.S. District Judge, 307-772-2104; William C. Beaman, U.S. Magistrate
Judge, 307-772-2895 The District of Wyoming Court is working with the Wyo-
ming State Bar Association to establish a court-sponsored mediation program.

1354025